CONTENTS

NOTE ON THE TEXT

The text comprises a complete transcription of the surviving portion of the diary of John Campbell, first cashier of The Royal Bank of Scotland, and runs from Saturday 14th September to Thursday 5th December 1745. The diary is primarily concerned with his business affairs and is in the form of an aide memoire of transactions and correspondence related to his role as both bank cashier and agent in Edinburgh of Lord Glenorchy.

The custodial history of the diary is not fully documented. Although it has formed part of the archive collection of The Royal Bank of Scotland for over a century, it may not have been held by the bank since Campbell's period of office. The diary was privately published in 1881, in a highly edited form, under the title *Leaves from the Diary of an Edinburgh Banker in 1745*. Only twenty copies of this edition were produced and, in order to make the manuscript more widely available, it was reprinted twelve years later by the Scottish History Society, in the first volume of *Miscellany of the Scottish History Society* (Edinburgh, 1893, pp.537-59). At that time the diary appears to have been in the possession of The Royal Bank of Scotland.

The diary is undoubtedly written in John Campbell's own hand, for the script matches entries in his private books of account, purchased by the Royal Bank from Sir Guy Campbell in 1974. It was a working document and seems to be a record of activities and events compiled concurrently rather than retrospectively. Many of the pages are closely written and Campbell uses such devices as doodles of pointing hands and marginal notes to indicate both things yet to be done and those which had been accomplished. The entries were clearly used by Campbell for the subsequent compilation of the minutes of the bank's court of directors.

The transcript, a verbatim rendering of the original manuscript diary, has been prepared in line with the following conventions:

- All words have been spelt exactly as in the diary.

- Abbreviated words have been silently extended as close to the modern spelling as written letters or marks of abbreviation allow, wherever this could be done with certainty. Extensions which are probable, but not certain, have been shown in square brackets.

- Modern usage of punctuation and capitalisation has been adopted.

- Marginalia has been indicated by angle brackets and interlineations incorporated in the body of the text.

- Words struck out, or erroneously duplicated by John Campbell, have been omitted.

- Illegible words or parts of words have been represented by three adjacent points.

- Spaces left for interpolations which were never made by John Campbell have been indicated by empty square brackets.

- Lengthy passages have been broken up into paragraphs for ease of reference, and an absence of any space between paragraphs indicates that they are part of a continuous narrative in the diary.

INTRODUCTION

John S Gibson

John Campbell was cashier to The Royal Bank of Scotland, at its
headquarters among the high tenements of old Edinburgh, from 1745 until
his death in 1777. He had joined the bank upon its foundation and worked
initially in the accountant's office. He was subsequently appointed assistant
secretary in 1732 and second cashier in 1734. Amongst the archival records
of The Royal Bank of Scotland can be found a portion of his diary, covering
the autumn months of 1745 which saw the descent of Prince Charles
Edward Stuart's army on Edinburgh and its occupation of the city, while
the Bonnie Prince himself held Court at Holyrood. These pages, which may
have been part of a career-long diary, raise the intriguing question of how
it came about that the Royal Bank, the government's bank, should have
come to finance the Highland Army, the rebel army, for the invasion
across the Border of November 1745? This march into England, was in
Dr Samuel Johnson's words, the 'noble attempt' to win back the throne of
Great Britain for the Stuarts which penetrated as far as Derby, then ebbed
back to Scotland, and so to ultimate defeat on Culloden Moor in April 1746.

It is not known why part of Campbell's diary has survived. Large excerpts
focusing on John Campbell's dealings with the Highland Army during the
occupation of Edinburgh were, however, published by the Scottish History
Society in 1893.[1] Their significance does not seem to have been fully
recognised at the time; Jacobite studies had then a long way to go. But
Walter Biggar Blaikie, doyen of Jacobite historians, in his contribution to
the *Book of the Old Edinburgh Club 1909*[2] on the events of 1745 in the city,
clearly did see their import. Since then, for all the veritable library that
has been written about the 'Forty-Five, this central question, why did the
Royal Bank help finance the Highland Army as it prepared for the invasion
of England, has gone unnoticed, or it has been treated half-humorously as
in Neil Munro's bi-centenary history of the Royal Bank of 1928[3], or passed
over as in Professor Checkland's more recent history of Scottish banking.[4]
Only in AW Kerr's *History of Banking in Scotland*, which predates these
two, is there curiosity expressed 'that the Government authorities should

have allowed the Prince thus to secure the sinews of war'[5]. The publication in full of Campbell's diary by the Royal Bank makes it possible to form a considered view of this puzzling matter, and on this the 250th anniversary of the last Jacobite Rising, it makes an important contribution to its history. It is an interesting tale, illustrative of Edinburgh attitudes towards King George and to the Prince's Highland Army alike; and Edinburgh of 1745 comes to life in John Campbell's pages.

By 1745 The Royal Bank of Scotland was eighteen years old. It had been founded in 1727 as a Whig enterprise in opposition to the Bank of Scotland, 'the Old Bank' as it was from then on popularly known. Its opponents rightly or wrongly had complained that 'the Old Bank' was slow to assist the development of Scotland by the advance of credit, and they put it about, with some reason, that its directors were tainted with Jacobitism. In its founding the Royal Bank had enjoyed powerful backing from the Duke of Argyll and his brother the Earl of Ilay, that duumvirate which had in effect ruled Scotland in the interests of the House of Hanover in the decades after the suppression of the great Jacobite rebellion of 1715. The bank's deputy governor who presided at meetings of its court of directors was the strong-minded, intensely political Lord Milton, Lord Justice Clerk by means of Argyll preferment, their 'man in Edinburgh' for the conduct of Scottish affairs, which in the early 1740's meant largely patronage for all posts in the government's gift. Bank business was conducted at the big building the Bank had taken over at the foot of Ship Close, sometimes subsequently known as Newbank Close, a house standing on its own with a garden and, when the reek of the city's chimneys cleared, views to the north over Bearford's Parks to the Firth and the shores of Fife beyond. Newbank Close led on to the north side of the High Street; and here, since it is germane to our story, some brief mention of the layout of the eighteenth century city is needed.

As, that summer of 1745, you walked up the steepness of Newbank Close, in perpetual twilight from the height of the tenements on either side known to Edinburgh people as 'lands', you debouched on to the High Street, Edinburgh's *grande place*. Here was a look of magnificence, travellers from the south would concede, as splendid as that of any town scene in Europe. The great street ran along the ridge which extended downhill from the Castle, dominated on either side by these tall lands housing all ranks

2

and conditions (and rats beyond number in the wainscoting) as if on the under-decks of a ninety-gun ship. Like roof-beams as seen from the ridge-pole, on either side of the High Street wynds and closes, abysses like Newbank Close between the high buildings, ran down on one side to the waters of the Nor' Loch and the noisome Flesh Market, on the other to a busy street, the Cowgate, in its ravine. Within the *grande place* the heart of the town lay around the building which had once been the great medieval church of St. Giles and was now quaintly divided into four Kirks. It was at one of these, called the New Church, that John Campbell worshipped every Sabbath. Close by were Goldsmith's Hall, where the Town Council met, and the laurel-wreathed statue of King Charles II (who never came to Edinburgh), and next to that the striking baroque building which in the years before the Union of 1707 had housed the Scottish Parliament. Beyond that was the grim Tolbooth, now the city's prison, which had been burst open by the Edinburgh mob eight years past to seize and lynch Captain Porteous of the City Guard.

Up the slope towards Edinburgh Castle the High Street led on to the Land Market ('the Lawnmarket' in Edinburgh pronunciation) from which the narrow, winding West Bow ran sharply downhill, giving the only street access from the city's main thoroughfare to the Cowgate and to the West Port, one of the six gates in the city's ancient walls, and so to the highway to the west. Downhill from St. Giles the High Street ran, past the burgh cross, past the Tron Kirk with its wooden Dutch steeple, past old houses with wooden galleries, curiously carved, towards the impressive turreted Netherbow Gate. Beyond this was the Canongate with its houses for gentry, mansions for nobility, and the Palace of Holyrood which for the past sixty years had been bereft of royalty, but where on an upper floor lived the aged 2nd Earl of Breadalbane, John Campbell's patron and chief.

Within its narrow compass, the Edinburgh of 1745 had a population thought to be approximately sixty thousand. Throughout the day, except on the Sabbath, all was bustle on the plainstanes and causeway of the *grande place*. The city's many taverns, such as Lucky Clerk's down Fleshmarket Close, John's coffee house in Parliament Close, and another in Writers Close much used by town councillors, were filled with gentry come to town, advocates and Writers to the Signet from Parliament House - and bank directors and officials from the big house down Newbank Close.

As evening came on, the noise in the street intensified, highland chairmen jostled with their sedan chairs, the main means of conveyance in the town, and used by John Campbell when visiting his aged chief at Holyrood. After dark there was the splash on the pavements of 'the most splendid street in Europe' of stinking slops decanted from the high lands. A city of contrasts indeed, for Edinburgh could now boast the finest public infirmary to be found in civilisation.

Over the whole town the historic Castle presided. Perhaps it was some premonition of civil disturbance which had led the Board of Ordnance in distant London to strengthen, within the past decade, the Castle's defences. A new house in the solid style of the period had been built for the Castle's governor. Now, in addition to the great gun platforms of the Half-Moon and Argyle batteries commanding the eastern approach, walls punctuated by pepper box turrets for sentries looked down on the Nor' Loch and on the green fields to the west.

* * *

John Campbell was a grandson of another John Campbell, *Iain Glas*, 'Pale John', the great 1st Earl of Breadalbane, 'cunning as a fox, wise as a serpent, slippery as an eel'[6], who from the Restoration of 1660 until the Jacobite Rising of 1715 had been the major force in highland politics as chief of the Breadalbane Campbells of Perthshire. The father to the John Campbell who became second cashier of the Royal Bank in 1734 was Colin Campbell of Ardmaddy (on the Argyllshire coast), the 1st Earl's third son. He died unmarried in 1708 while John Campbell was still a child, but illegitimacy was no bar to preferment. The 2nd Earl was an important aristocratic customer of the new-established Royal Bank; either through his influence or that of Lord Glenorchy his heir, John Campbell obtained his post there. It happening that Alan Whitefoord, the Bank's chief official, soon fell into bad health, for many years before 1745 John Campbell had been in effective charge at the Newbank House down Newbank Close.

One further comment on John Campbell which would also apply to all his Edinburgh contemporaries, be they Lord Milton, Lord Justice Clerk in

Parliament House who was the Bank's deputy governor, the 2nd Earl of
Breadalbane in his apartment at Holyrood, Lord Provost Archibald
Stewart the city's chief magistrate, or the waiter at Lucky Clerk's, is that
they all spoke broad Scots, however precise the written English of the first
four of these might be.

What then are John Campbell's political sympathies likely to have been in
those years after the suppression of the 'Fifteen when Scotland found that
she had as King the Elector of Hanover, 'the wee, wee German lairdie' of
Jacobite song? There should have been no doubt about this. The Royal
Bank was the Whig bank as opposed to its older rival, the Bank of Scotland
down Old Bank Close off the southern side of the Lawnmarket, with its
supposed Jacobite associations. On the establishment of the Royal Bank in
1727, Lord Milton, as deputy governor, had arranged that the Royal Bank
should be the channel through which the army in Scotland was paid as it
garrisoned fortresses and thrust new military roads through the
Grampians. The Royal Bank, again through Lord Milton's influence, was
also the route for payment of such other government expenditure as found
its way to King George's North Britain. From his country house on the
road to Musselburgh and his town house down the Canongate, Lord Milton,
Lord Justice Clerk, was a firm hand on the tiller of government in Scotland
and of the Royal Bank alike.

Then, to reinforce Whig influence on the Royal Bank, there was Lord
Glenorchy, heir to the 2nd Earl of Breadalbane. To Lord Glenorchy John
Campbell, in addition to his post as the Royal Bank's chief official, acted as
'man of business' in Edinburgh. Lord Glenorchy, who by 1745 had long
replaced his now octogenarian father in the conduct of the clan's affairs,
was wholly Hanoverian in interests and outlook. As far back as 1718, two
years after the collapse of the 'Fifteen, he had a place of importance at the
Hanoverian court as Master of the Horse to the beautiful, energetic and
influential Caroline, Princess of Wales. This had been followed, while he
was still only twenty-five years old, by his appointment as minister at
Copenhagen, and in 1731 as ambassador at St. Petersburg. On revival of
the Order in 1725 he had been made a Knight of the Bath; and he was a
strong supporter of Walpole in the decades when Sir Robert, by fair means
or foul, dominated Westminster and damned all Jacobites. The 2nd Earl's
heir, who had equipped himself with a wife from the English Whig

aristocracy, clearly calculated that the future lay with the House of
Hanover. So, one might imagine, and perhaps imagine wrongly, had John
Campbell. For it has to be recognised that for Lord Glenorchy to have gone
over so openly to supporting the House of Hanover had been a political
volte-face for the Breadalbane Campbells.

In the great Jacobite Rising of 1715, *Iain Glas*, the aged 1st Earl, had sent
seven hundred of his clan to fight for the Stuart Cause. At the Battle of
Sheriffmuir in November 1715, seemingly inconclusive as it was but a
check from which the Jacobite cause did not recover, the Breadalbane
regiment, brigaded with Clan Donald (all memories laid aside of the
infamous part their Glenlyon men had played in the Massacre of Glencoe),
had swept away the right wing of the Royal Army. The Clan Donald bards
were to celebrate the prowess of the Breadalbane Campbells in the songs
they made about the battle, and it was a proud memory for the clan itself.
Iain Glas died just after the collapse of the 'Fifteen, and in all likelihood
thereby saved the earldom from attainder. His son who succeeded as 2nd
Earl, though imprisoned for a while for his part in the 'Fifteen, escaped
punishment, perhaps through the influence of his Campbell kinsman,
the Duke of Argyll, who had led the Royal Army at Sheriffmuir. The
Breadalbane Clan and their chief now kept their heads below the parapet.
Unlike their neighbours the Murrays of Atholl, they took no part in the
Jacobite Rising of 1719 which came to nothing. Thereafter the 2nd Earl,
then entering old age, concentrated on his estates, though from 1737 he was
nominally one of the Scottish representative peers at Westminster. But
there would be many gentry along Loch Tay-side and among the Perthshire
hills who were still Jacobite at heart.

It was among these Breadalbane gentry that John Campbell grew to
manhood at the clan's stronghold of Finlarig at the western end of Loch
Tay. One such was the now elderly Patrick Campbell of Monzie - Monzie in
the hills above Crieff - who as a Breadalbane Campbell had been Jacobite
in 1715, and had notably exerted himself in the years after the 'Fifteen on
behalf of the 'rebels'. Patrick Campbell was now Lord Monzie, a judge at
the Court of Session and, the Breadalbane influence again apparent, a
director at the Royal Bank. Another Breadalbane Campbell with whom
John Campbell was in frequent communication was John Campbell of
Auchalader, the 2nd Earl's elderly and much respected chamberlain at

Auchmore near to Finlarig. His memories too would have been of the great days of *Iain Glas* and Jacobite loyalty. Perhaps too, as we will see, some vestige of Jacobite sentiment, if not loyalty, remained in the 2nd Earl himself.

For indeed by 1745 sentiment, and religion as well for so many in the Episcopalian north-east and among the Catholic clans, still induced a strong desire to see 'the auld Stewarts back again'. Scotland was split, or rather it contained a confusion of opinion on the matter. Those such as Lord Milton who had prospered with the dominance of the House of Argyll; military men in King George's service such as General George Preston, the governor of Edinburgh Castle; almost every minister of the Church of Scotland and the ultra-devout members of their flocks who saw Hanoverian rule as the guarantee of the maintenance of 'true religion'; Glasgow merchants now beginning to grasp the new opportunities offered by the Union in the Virginia tobacco trade; all these were resolute for King George II. But according to a contemporary and well-informed history of the 'Forty-Five written from the Whig point of view, in Edinburgh disaffection with London rule, merging into active Jacobitism, was rife in legal and mercantile circles alike. In Edinburgh, wrote this as yet unidentified author in 1747, 'writers, agents, attorneys, clerks and procurators (not to say advocates and lawyers)' had been infected with Jacobitism in the years before the Rising[7]. Town magistrates and office bearers in the main 'of a low descent, mean education, little knowledge and small substance', their fortunes bound up with the maintenance of the vigorous smuggling industry, were all too easily swayed by the Jacobites. Edinburgh's self-electing Town Council was split. Ex-Lord Provost George Drummond, an important man in the town, was a resolute Whig who had fought for King George at Sheriffmuir; but Archibald Stewart, the current Lord Provost from a family of Perthshire Stewarts, was widely reputed to be Jacobite. The Reverend Alexander Carlyle, luminary of Edinburgh's Enlightenment in the later decades of the century, a lifelong Whig and pillar of the established order, who in September 1745 had joined Sir John Cope's army as a young volunteer on the march which ended so disastrously in a field of corn-stubble near Prestonpans, would in his old age write this significant comment on the political divide as he had seen it in his youth: 'The Commons in General, as well as two-thirds of the Gentry, at that period, had no aversion to the Family of Stuart, and could their Religion have been Secur'd, would have been very glad to see them on the Throne again'.[8]

Where, in 1745, might John Campbell have stood amid all this political uncertainty? He had his own residence at the village of Restalrig a couple of miles east of Edinburgh where, if Duncan Bàn MacIntyre the Gaelic poet who was later so to eulogise him is to be believed, he was a great dispenser of hospitality. But politically he was an enigma. Except perhaps for this. In 1749, only three years after an Act of the Westminster Parliament in the repressive legislation that followed the 'Forty-Five had made illegal the wearing of highland dress by anyone, anywhere, John Campbell had his portrait painted. It hangs today in the boardroom of the Royal Bank's offices in Edinburgh at 36 St Andrew Square. This portrait is remarkable, not only for the splendid depiction of Campbell's genial and handsome features, but also for this - he chose to be painted magnificently swathed in tartan.

Above all, John Campbell was a Highlander.

* * *

The 'Forty-Five did not fall on King George's 'North Britain' out of a clear blue sky. Great Britain had been involved in European war since 1742 and 'The Concert of Gentlemen', representative of Highland and Lowland Jacobites, had since 1741 been involved in secret treaty obligations with France. Send across the six thousand of your famous Irish Brigade, the compact with Louis XV's ministers ran, and we will raise twenty thousand Scots to join them against King George. By 1745, word of this would have come to the ears of many, the more so since it had come close to activation the previous year when French military might seriously threatened an audacious cross-Channel invasion to the Sussex coast. Nor would an Edinburgh citizen have been unaware of the Jacobite roystering in February 1745, to mark the birthday of the younger son of the exiled Jacobite king. All that summer Lord President Duncan Forbes, and Lord Milton as Lord Justice Clerk, had been watchful. In May King George's army in Flanders had suffered a heavy reverse at French hands at the Battle of Fontenoy; and in early June, Lord Milton had had scooped up from his Canongate lodging and incarcerated in Edinburgh Castle Sir Hector Maclean, newcome from France with secret orders for the Scottish Jacobites.

It was, however, something of a shock when on the 8th of August a communication reached Edinburgh from the Marquis of Tweeddale, the Secretary of State for Scotland in distant London, that there was imminent prospect of a Franco-Jacobite descent on Scotland. It was followed the next day by news from the Argyllshire Campbells that Charles Edward Stuart, the exiled king's elder son, had now landed in the West Highlands and was raising some sort of an army from the Jacobite clans.

There followed the hurried despatch of Sir John Cope, commander-in-chief of King George's forces in Scotland, with his guns and two thousand infantry to smother what the Lord President (wishfully) described as a 'fire of straw'. Then Cope, outmanoeuvred among the hills, made for Inverness, leaving the new-built military road to the south open to Prince Charles Edward's small army. On the last day of August word came to Edinburgh that the Prince was in the Braes of Athole; four days later that Perth had fallen. On Saturday 14th September a horseman brought the long-feared news from Perth; the Highland Army had resumed its southward progress. In quick succession there came further intelligence. The Highland Army was now across the Forth, outwith the guns of Stirling Castle; was marching on Edinburgh; was already at Linlithgow. In Edinburgh volunteers assembled for the city's defence with muskets sent down from the Castle; the ancient city walls were manned after a fashion; and two dragoon regiments in scarlet and gold positioned themselves to the west of Edinburgh along the Water of Leith to confront the approaching threat.

* * *

Breaking the Sabbath calm in Edinburgh, Lord Milton presiding, the Royal Bank's directors had first considered the threat from the north when they met at the bank house on Sunday 1st September. The minute of that meeting records that they had before them 'certain intelligence' (which proved premature) that the Highland Army was already on the march from Perth. It was agreed that, to keep it out of rebel hands, the Bank's reserves of gold and silver, with all the Bank's papers, be transported to a place of security. Likewise, lest they should get into the wrong (Jacobite) hands, a start was made to the contraction of credit by the calling-in of bank notes;

and £10,600 of these were destroyed. Directors were from then on to meet every day, twice if need be; and keeping a wary eye on their rivals down Old Bank Close, they resolved to stop trading as soon as the Bank of Scotland did so. For their part, the Bank of Scotland was still more energetic in restricting credit in the face of the Highland Army's advance, reducing the volume of their notes in circulation by over £140,000 or forty per cent.

In the fortnight that followed, all was got ready for a move of the Bank's effects to the safety of Edinburgh Castle. It was as well. The minute of the directors' meeting for 14th September - Lord Milton still presiding - reads:

> *On information that the highland Army is on the march towards this city; the directors ... judging that in this exigency it is not proper to let ... [the Bank's treasure, books and other effects] remain in the office as it is not a place of strength to hold out against an attack, or any insult: and having got notice that the old Bank have this evening conveyed their valuable effects to the Castle of Edinburgh and lodged them in Major Roberton's House... Resolved ... that the whole gold and silver coin, banknotes, struck and unstruck, together with all the Old Bank notes ... and in general everything that may be of any value or real use be forthwith packt up in boxes and immediately transported to the Castle of Edinburgh and lodged in the place viewed some days agoe...*

'Which being done', the minute concludes, 'every box was marked and carried off to the carts upon the street'. It then lists what was lugged up Newbank Close to the waiting carts on the High Street. An iron chest with £14,000 in gold. Six boxes of silver each with £1,000. A box with £47,600 in bank notes. Another box with £13,700 in Royal Bank notes. Two boxes of plate which had been lodged as security for loans. A bag of half guineas. Eight bags of silver each of £100. £6,200 worth of Royal Bank twenty shilling notes. All this and 'plate of Lord Glenorchy's which was in the hands of John Campbell cashier as his Lordship's Doer [man of business] and which at my Lady Glenorchy's desire [she at this time in England] he sends along with the Bank things to a place of security'. To watch over all this hoard, George Innes, the Bank's chief teller, was 'to ly in the vault

where the Bank things are deposited'. He took his wife with him: it could
be a long stay.

And so the Bank closed its doors.

* * *

It is at this point that the surviving pages of John Campbell's diary begin.
The diary is in the nature of a register of correspondence and record of
financial transactions at this time of crisis, with mention interspersed about
the Jacobite occupation of Edinburgh. Here was a busy man endeavouring
to keep Lord Glenorchy and the Perthshire lairds, Lady Glenorchy in
London as well, informed of the course of events; he dines regularly with
the old Earl of Breadalbane in his apartment on the upper floor at
Holyrood, while the Prince holds court on the floor below. The centrepiece
of it all is his meticulous record of the events involving the Highland
Army's demand to the Royal Bank for money, and of the circumstances in
which Edinburgh Castle, while under Jacobite siege, was prevailed on to
yield up golden guineas to meet that demand. But on that September
Saturday Campbell had no time to make anything but the briefest of entries:

Saturday 14 September 1745

On news of the highland army's approach, all the effects of the
Bank were packt up, and partly transported to the C[astle] this
night per memorandum apart. Lord G[lenorchy]'s boxes likewise
transported. Paid sundrys to workmen for the Bank ...

The rest of the boxes and bags went up to the Castle the following day.
This Sunday, the 15th, was the day when the volunteers assembled on the
Grassmarket that they might march out of the West Port to fight in support
of the two regiments of dragoons at the Colt Bridge on the Water of Leith -
but thought better of it. On Monday 16th September, Brigadier-General
Fowkes, newly arrived from England to take charge, rightly judged that
without supporting infantry the dragoons could not take on the Highlanders,
and ordered a retreat to join with Sir John Cope's army, now believed to

be approaching the Firth of Forth from Aberdeen in naval transports.
This retreat of ill-disciplined cavalry streaming along the fields on the
far side of the Nor' Loch, abandoning Edinburgh to its fate, was watched
from the bank house. 'Saw the Dragoons run óff along the north side of
Edinburgh', wrote Campbell in his diary, 'The town in a consternation all
day. Volunteers arms deliverd in to the Castle on allarm of the firebell in
the evening ... Deputation of the Magistracy sent out to Bellsmilns
[Slateford, on the Water of Leith] to capitulate with the P as to the surrender
of the town'.

His entry for the following day, the 17th of September, about the storming
of the Netherbow Gate by a force of Lochiel's Camerons and of Clan
Donald is similarly factual: 'Edinburgh taken by the highland army 1200
men sent in early in the morning... Sundry proclamations over the Cross.
Prince enters Holyroodhouse'. Here, for the first time, Campbell refers to
Charles Edward as 'the Prince' instead of 'the P' (which could be read as
Prince or Pretender). It is in marked distinction from that other diarist
and avid Whig in Edinburgh in the 'Forty-Five, Patrick Crichton[9], a
Grassmarket saddler and ironmonger, to whom Charles Edward is at best
'the Pretended Prince' but usually referred to in terms of greater hostility
with all Highlanders termed derisively 'scurlewheelers' or 'hillskipers', and
who watched (as perhaps also did John Campbell, emerging from Newbank
Close) the proclamation in dead silence of 'King James the Eight' at the
Mercat Cross in the High Street by Roderick Chalmers, Ross Herald, in his
emblazoned tabard, followed by wild cheering from the huge crowd, a great
blowing of Clan Cameron's bagpipes, every window in the high lands all
around 'full of Ladys who threw up their handkerchiefs, and clap'd their
hands and show'd great loyalty to the Bonnie Prince', as one young lady
described the scene.[10]

In succeeding days, as he would do throughout the Jacobite occupation,
Campbell would send copies of the profoundly Jacobite, thrice-weekly,
Caledonian Mercury, rather than the Whig *Edinburgh Evening Courant*,
to Lord Glenorchy, then at Ardmaddy, but subsequently at Taymouth
Castle in Strathtay; to Lady Glenorchy in London; to Campbell of
Auchalader and to Lord Monzie, both in Perthshire. On Monday 23rd
September the *Mercury* gave a full and ecstatic account of the Jacobite
victory over Cope at Prestonpans on the 21st. Campbell's diary noted with

apparent satisfaction the *Mercury's* 'serious reflections' on the battle 'that 2,000 highland foot, unsupported by horse and charged in front and flank with artillery and small arms, routed a regular army of above 4,000 horse and foot in an open plain and obtained a most signal and compleat victory with a very inconsiderable loss'. There would be no Breadalbane Regiment in this Jacobite Rising. The fiery cross had, literally, gone round Loch Tayside, but in vain: Lord Glenorchy had seen to that. However their neighbours from Glenlyon were coming out, and Stewarts and Murrays aplenty from Atholl. Did this stir John Campbell's highland pride?

By the morning of Sunday 22nd September a few officers of Cope's army and about a hundred other escapees from the carnage of the battle had found refuge in Edinburgh Castle. Their arrival, with wildly exaggerated estimates of the strength of the army which had overwhelmed them, did nothing to stiffen the resolve of General Guest who had been left there in overall command. A kindly Yorkshireman who had risen from the ranks early on in Marlborough's wars, Joshua Guest was now all of eighty-five years old, an invalid scarcely able to stir from his room, living off a milk diet and reputedly with something of Jacobite sympathy in his past. With the approach of the Highland Army he had been in a flutter, begging advice from the Lord Milton about what to do - and the latter was now with Cope at Berwick, whither 'Johnny' Cope had fled after the catastrophe to his army at Prestonpans. Also at Berwick was Lord Mark Kerr, the Castle's sinecure governor. The deputy governor, who <u>was</u> at his post, was General George Preston, another veteran of King William's and Marlborough's wars, and like Guest an octogenarian. Preston, however, had been the Castle's deputy governor for thirty years and, unlike Guest, who was the son of an ostler, he was 'of family' with all the self-assurance that implied, the Prestons of Valleyfield in Fife tracing their descent deep into mediaeval times The deputy governor's influence would be crucial. According to the story Robert Chambers, the great nineteenth century antiquary had, and believed, from an old lady of Preston's family, Guest, as shocked as the new arrivals at Cope's defeat, was for giving up the Castle, maintaining that its garrison was unfit to withstand the rigours of a siege by an army as strong in numbers as the Highlanders were (wrongly) reputed to be. Preston, with a sharper appreciation of what King George's interests required, would have none of this.[11]

This 22nd of September was another Edinburgh Sabbath, and as John Campbell noted in his diary the city's kirks were silent, the ministers of the established Church having astutely taken themselves out of town; reckoning that nothing would bring the city's population to its senses more quickly than being denied its weekly dosage of Calvinism. However, it was to general acclamation from the Edinburgh mob and the more respectable alike that on the evening of this day, the Prince returned to Edinburgh, his army's pipers blazing away at *The King shall enjoy his own again.*

* * *

Victory at Prestonpans was a false crest. The immediate advance into England, which the Prince so ardently wished, was out of the question for the present, the common Highlanders' age-old custom of returning to their glens to 'stash' their booty after victory won, a telling comment on the poverty in which so many lived, had for a while sorely depleted the strength of the Highland Army. The persuasion of Sir Alexander MacDonald of Sleat, MacLeod at Dunvegan in Skye and that aged octogenarian Lord Lovat to bring out their followings for the Cause and so augment the Prince's army was the immediate need; this, and the creation of confidence among the citizenry as to how their new masters would conduct themselves. To this end, as Campbell's diary notes, a proclamation from Holyrood enjoined the banks, in the Prince's name, to reopen for business. It spoke of the 'great inconvenience' that had attended the removal of the banks' reserves into the Castle, and of the current 'false rumours' that the Prince intended to seize money whenever it was found. 'The money lodged in the banks should be entirely under his protection', the Prince's proclamation ran, 'free from all contribution to be exacted in time coming so that the banks might return to their former business in safety'.

The banks remained shut. Ominously for them, this Holyrood proclamation also spoke of the Prince's intention to issue bank notes of his own 'for the re-establishment of public credit'. It was known that the Jacobites had a mobile printing press. The fear was that the country would either be swamped with counterfeit notes, or a new paper currency which could be exchanged for Royal Bank and Bank of Scotland notes, and so raise the demand for specie.

Money for the Highland Army was the other pressing need. Along with the
baggage of the Royal Army, Cope's military chest of £4,000 had been
seized. A half-a-crown levy on every pound sterling of Edinburgh rentals
would shortly be imposed, Newbank House, as John Campbell noted,
bearing its share to pay for tents for the Prince's army. But this would not
be enough. It was imperative that the Prince be able to continue to pay his
rank and file the requisite sixpence a day, much more for the clanned
gentry. Were the Highland Army to attempt to live off the country in line
with the worst practices of continental armies, they would soon lose the
popularity they as yet enjoyed. In the Prince's mind there was, too, the
need for money in the form of golden guineas, rather than alien Scottish
banknotes, to make possible the invasion of England he so ardently
desired. So John Hay of Restalrig (a neighbour of John Campbell),
Jacobite son of an Edinburgh Writer to the Signet, was dispatched with an
armed escort to Glasgow, then enjoying a new prosperity from the tobacco
trade with Virginia, to exact monies from that town's Bailie Nicol Jarvies.

On the 29th of September John Hay was back from Glasgow with £5,500,
that town's reluctant contribution to the Prince's military chest. But some
of this was not in coin but in Royal Bank of Scotland notes, and so two
days later there was a call at Newbank Close from John Murray of Broughton,
the Prince's Secretary; and at this point Campbell's diary, which had up to
then been mainly in the nature of an aide memoire of his own correspondence
and transactions, expands to a full account of his dealings with the Jacobite
Army for subsequent entry in the Bank's minute book.

> *Between 6 and 7 a clock at night a protest was then taken against*
> *me, as Cashier of the R[oyal] Bank by John Murray of Broughton*
> *esquire as Secretary to the Prince for payment of £857 Royal*
> *Bank notes, (which he exhibited) in the current coin of the kingdom,*
> *and on failzure thereof within 48 hours, that the estates and effects*
> *of the directors and managers should be distressed for the same.*

Campbell replied that this was an impossible request as all of the Bank's
moneys were lodged in Edinburgh Castle, and the governor there was
denying access. Campbell went on to explain that four days past he and
two of the Bank's directors wishing to conduct banking business (i.e. the
destruction of bank notes in the face of the Jacobite threat to print their

own currency) had been refused entry to the Castle 'though they continued at the gate for about an hour'. Murray was adamant. He would give him, in the Prince's name, a pass through the Jacobite lines now watching the Castle Hill. He hoped that the governor would give admittance. But whether he did or not, if the payment was not made the order would be put into execution, and the directors' homes, with his own house at Restalrig, 'distressed'. Thereupon, at Mrs Clerk's tavern down Fleshmarket Close, Campbell met the only two directors still in town, Lord Milton, as mentioned above, having taken himself off a fortnight past, and they agreed to meet again at Newbank House at 9 next morning 'that this affair might be further concerted, and if possible money might be got out for answering the demand'. Meanwhile a letter should be sent to Lieutenant General Guest seeking access, after its terms had been approved by Murray of Broughton 'to prevent all mistake' (presumably any disclosure of the real purpose of the intended visit), and the other Bank directors should be notified. Today it is argued by some, that the Laird of Broughton had a right to demand that the bank notes be honoured - but could one who was in open rebellion against King George claim the protection of his laws?

When they convened the following morning there was a message from Murray of Broughton that there would shortly be a further demand on the Bank, and when they dined at Mrs Clerk's later that day the lawyer Peter Smith, brother of the Perthshire laird Smith of Methven, presented himself on behalf of the Prince's Secretary. Calling Campbell to another room at Lucky Clerk's he said that there was now a further £2,307 in bank notes to be converted into specie and that this must be done within forty-eight hours. (The Royal Bank had, it seems, not been as quick as their rival the Bank of Scotland in withdrawing notes from circulation in the days before the arrival of the Highland Army). This further demand the directors agreed had to be accepted, though Campbell says he expostulated to Smith:

> ....upon the impossibility of the thing but he [Peter Smith] said
> that all excuse was in vain, for that a gentleman, who understood
> the business of banking, was with the Prince, ... who said that
> there was no difficulty in the thing, for that all the gold and silver
> must be in baggs of certain sums, and therefore that it was an
> easy matter, and required no great time to execute this affair, and
> so the Prince was positive to grant no longer indulgence.

Over a pot of coffee at Muirhead's coffee house John Campbell continued discussion with Philp and his fellow directors. Their fears would not be simply over the practicability of bringing the moneys out. They were also about their own safety in seeking access to the Bank's reserves lodged in the Castle. For the Castle itself, now under siege, was firing on the town.

It may have had been a measure of the frustration now gripping the Prince and his Council that, in default of knowing what to do next after victory at Prestonpans, they should now have chosen to harass Edinburgh Castle. On their return to Edinburgh on the evening of 22nd September they had posted guards from Lochiel's Camerons in the Grassmarket, and in the Weigh House at the head of the Lawnmarket to which in more normal times in this well-regulated municipality traders in butter and cheese brought their produce. But until now the sentries had not sought to interfere with the passage of supplies for the Castle garrison. What now lit the fuse may have been old General Preston's response from the Castle to the Prince's demand that he instruct Captain Beavor of His Majesty's twenty-four-gun frigate the *Fox* and the twenty-gun *Happy Jennet*, now in the Firth of Forth, to refrain from obstructing Jacobite movement on the ferry across the Forth to Kinghorn and at the Queensferry: the doughty old General had replied that he would rather grant a pass to Hell to any Jacobite who applied!

On the evening of 29 September a letter from the Castle came to the Lord Provost at his house at the head of the narrow winding West Bow: unless communication between the Castle and the town was kept open the Castle's cannon would fire to dislodge the highland guards; and the Castle's guns would 'distress' the city if it did not furnish provisions for the garrison. As Campbell's diary records, a town meeting of sorts was there and then called to the 'New Church' within the walls of old St. Giles; and next morning six deputies from the Town Council waited on the Prince at Holyrood to show him the general's letter. Charles Edward gave them a reply in writing to take up to the Castle saying that 'he was equally surprised and concerned' at the barbarity of the intention of 'bringing distress on the town'. If the threat was carried out he would see to it that General Preston's house of Valleyfield was likewise distressed. This reply in turn was conveyed to the Castle by the Town Council's anxious deputies, evoking the immediate response from the old warrior there that the guns of

His Majesty's frigate, the *Fox*, would be turned on the Jacobite Lord Elcho's cliff-top Wemyss Castle - also on the coast of Fife - should Valleyfield suffer. In this strange civil war of a sort the generals did, however, agree to a six-day truce for instructions to be sought from London as to any draconian measures of retaliation on the town.

But before a reply could be received the truce broke down. A supply of butter into the Castle for the ailing Guest's stomach had been allowed by Murray of Broughton, until a smuggled letter - perhaps from the Captain of *HMS Fox* - was found concealed in the cask. On the afternoon of 1 October the highland sentries at the Weigh House fired in *terrorem* on people carrying provisions to the Castle. Straightaway the Castle's guns responded with both cannon and small shot, damaging houses on the Castle Hill which the Highlanders had occupied, wounding some of them and also a hapless servant-lass. Next day, the 2nd October, the Prince had a proclamation put up all over town forbidding on pain of death any communication between town and castle.

It was in the middle of this escalating violence that John Campbell, with his small group of Bank directors and colleagues, had to seek access to the Castle that they might attempt to meet the Highland Army's demands for coin. But first they equipped themselves with a pass through the guards at the Weigh House, obtained by meeting, at Mrs Clerk's tavern, with Cameron of Lochiel in his new found role as Jacobite Governor of Edinburgh. On the morning of 3rd October the little band, led by Campbell waving a white flag, made their way through the Cameron guards and into the Castle.

> *On our arrival at General Guest's lodgings, (which is the Governor's new house) the directors and I went in, told him our errand in general was to get in to the R[oyal] Bank repositories to do some business, and General Preston having come in at that instant, he was likewise told the same. After some short conversation we left the two generalls and proceeded to the place where all the Bank things are lodged, and executed the affairs we came about.*

'To do some business', they said, hiding the fact, it seems, that their purpose - as well as the burning of Royal Bank notes - was to 'bank-roll' the Highland Army.

The excitements of the day were not yet over. For the six hours of their stay in the Castle there was the noise of cannonade on 'Livingston's yeards', a house in the open fields near the West Church (the present-day St. Cuthberts), where a Jacobite outpost had been positioned to prevent supplies being hoisted to the beleaguered garrison up the Castle's steep eastern cliffs. The Bank party saw the return of 'one Watson a soldier' who was let down these cliffs by rope when he surprised the Jacobite outpost, single-handedly killed several, set the house on fire and returned with the help of his rope into the Castle, 'where he was received with loud huzzars for his valour'. As they left the Castle, Campbell and his friends saw a sally forming which was to complete Watson's good work.

Campbell's diary entry for this momentous day continues:

> *Before I went to dinner* [at Lucky Clerk's] *I waited upon Mr John Murray of Broughton esquire* [this would be at Holyrood] *and told him I was come from the directors to acquaint him that they were ready to exchange current coin for their notes, in terms and in consequence of the two sealed demands made upon the Bank by way of protests and certification. On which he appointed six a clock at night to receive the money at my house.*

There the money was handed over to Andrew Lumisdean, Murray's young depute-secretary:

> *And so we parted about eleven a clock at night; having drunk one bottle of wine during our business. ... The net sum paid was £3076...*

This then is the essence of John Campbell's crucially important diary entry for 3rd October. In the next few weeks, to anticipate, Campbell would hand over to Murray of Broughton and his minions a further £3,600 in gold coin from the moneys they had brought down. Multiply these figures around eighty times for present day values. In the Prince's mind the invasion of England was now becoming possible.

For years after, every detail of the siege of Edinburgh Castle was to be discussed again and again round Edinburgh dinner tables. John Home, who as a leading-light of Edinburgh's literati was to compile a carefully researched *History of the Rebellion in the Year 1745*[12] (in which he had fought for King George), would assert there as fact that the generals' whole purpose throughout was to deter the Highland Army's southward departure from Edinburgh, in view of the pressing danger to King George and his ministers that this would coincide with a cross-channel invasion by France's huge army. Such an invasion had been close to embarkation at the beginning of the previous year, and it would be all but undertaken by King Louis' renowned Irish Brigade and other troops under Saxe's command in the months ahead. Home also cited an elaborate plan of disinformation put out by General Preston, which was intended to give the Prince's Council the false impression that the Castle's supplies were running low and consequently that surrender was imminent, and so ensure a prolongation of the Highland Army's stay in Edinburgh in the vain hope of bringing about by starvation that which want of siege guns had prevented happening by assault in early September.

Had General Preston known the destination of the specie now uplifted from the Castle, he would surely have sent John Campbell and his colleagues away empty-handed, if indeed he had not clapped them in the Castle's prison. It would also seem to have been a simple matter for Campbell, once inside the Castle, to have privately alerted the generals to the real purpose of the mission and the pressure being put on him by the Laird of Broughton and his men, and to have engineered a flat refusal from General Preston to allow any specie to be taken out. As to possible Jacobite 'distressing' of the properties of Bank directors and officials, including Lord Milton's town and country houses, such threats may have been alarming enough (although the Bank's minute book, unlike Campbell's diary, speaks not of 'distressing' but rather of mere 'occupation'). Peter Smith, Murray of Broughton's subordinate who conveyed them, was a sinister individual. He would later in the course of the Rising show the vile side of his nature by proposing in all seriousness that the thumbs of prisoners taken from King George's armies should be hacked off to prevent them re-engaging, should they escape their highland guards. One of the two Bank directors present on this escapade to the Castle was John Philp of Greenlaw, a Midlothian laird who had been a director of the Bank since its inception.

Philp, who seems to have been an ultra-cautious individual, may have feared the quartering of highland 'banditti' at handsome Greenlaw off the Peebles road. But as a highland gentleman John Campbell must have recognised that these threats to the properties of his directors and himself were hollow. The Prince could not afford so massively to antagonise opinion, let alone invite retaliation from the Castle or by the Royal Navy, such as had been threatened against Lord Elcho's pile at Wemyss.

What then is to be made of this two-fold 'transgression' on the part of John Campbell and his directors, firstly, in acceding at all in such an apparently weak-kneed fashion to Murray of Broughton's demand, and then once inside the Castle in apparently deceiving the generals as to 'the business' they wished to conduct. Was it simply a matter of canny Scots putting the safety of their own houses first, however dire the consequences of the invasion of England might be for King George's government? But as an earl's grandson and the Bank's chief official, John Campbell's voice would have been dominant over those of the two directors who accompanied him to the Castle. Was it, on the other hand, that Campbell and his directors were Jacobites of a sort, or - Scotland having no great reason to love the Georges - at best indifferent to the interests of the House of Hanover. But it seems unlikely they would, on their own, have flouted what we may take to have been the known wishes of Lord Milton, that staunch Hanoverian, the Bank's deputy governor and chairman of the court of directors.

This aspect of the history of the Rising has so far been little noticed, though, as mentioned at the outset, eighty-six years ago Walter Biggar Blaikie confessed to being deeply puzzled by these, as he put it, 'grotesque' events.[13] So, one wonders if there is here a trail that leads back to the apartment on the upper floor of Holyrood. As his diary records, Campbell was frequently in the old Earl's company throughout the six weeks of Jacobite occupation, and in the week following the Prince's triumphant return to Edinburgh from the battle of Prestonpans that erstwhile Jacobite the 2nd Earl of Breadalbane, in his apartment at the Palace, received a visit from the Prince himself.

We cannot know for certain, but the late Sir James Fergusson of Kilkerran, that most distinguished of Scottish historians, in his classic *Argyll in the*

'*Forty-Five*[14] suspected that in these heady days after the Prince's victory at Prestonpans, like so many of the Scottish nobility, the 2nd Earl's loyalties were swithering. Campbell's diary, now for the first time printed in full, shows for 4th October the receipt of a letter from Lord Glenorchy at Taymouth instructing him 'to make out proxies [relating to the voting in the House of Lords] for Earl of Breadalbane to sign' and send to Lady Glenorchy in London, for onward transmission to Lord Chancellor Hardwicke. The diary entry for the following day records Campbell's compliance with the instruction, and, after dining with the Earl at Holyrood, his sending the proxies off southwards. What fuelled Sir James' suspicions was his finding in the Breadalbane Papers the draft of a letter, dated 5th October, to the Lord Chancellor pleading that 'the loss of use of my arms and legs' made travel to London impossible. But this draft letter was written in Lord Glenorchy's unmistakeable hand, and he was still at Taymouth on that date. Did this, Sir James wondered, in the face of the old Earl's consorting with Jacobites at Holyrood, represent a filial attempt to prevail on his father to give some flimsy testimony of loyalty to the House of Hanover?

Again to anticipate events: what happened to the 'culprits' when the Jacobite army departed and Lord Milton returned to Edinburgh is just as strange, for the answer is 'nothing'. That payment in specie to the Prince's men was being made by the Royal Bank was quickly known. The *Scots Magazine* for September 1745, published in the early days of October mentions this, though the origin of the golden guineas so handed over was not. If, in the absence of Lord Milton, the payments were made on the advice of the old Earl at Holyrood, there would be an obvious need to cover up such an awkward fact and such treasonable conduct by Lord Glenorchy's father. On the other hand, the determining factor may have been fear of the acute embarrassment disclosure would have meant for Lord Milton, as Lord Justice Clerk, the effective head of civil government in Scotland in that winter of 1745. Or it may well have been that with the eyes of their competitor the Bank of Scotland upon them, the need for the Royal Bank to cover up its reluctant or otherwise 'bank-rolling' of the Highland Army worked in Campbell's favour and that of his directors. For Campbell, a long, distinguished and apparently untroubled career as the Bank's cashier was to follow, even though the Bank's deputy governor, Lord Milton, had let it be known that he 'found fault with almost every part of the directors' conduct' during his own enforced absence.

In the sour aftermath of the 'Forty-Five the Lord Provost of Edinburgh, whose conduct had in fact been almost blameless, was shut up in the Tower of London for a year and then had to stand trial for his supposed treason over the taking of the city by the Highland Army in September of 1745. On the basis of this and of all the evidence here presented, and from his own knowledge of eighteenth century Scotland, Lord Cameron, the now retired judge, observes that John Campbell may well be thought fortunate in escaping any retribution from Hanoverian authority for his part in giving aid and support in the form of hard cash to King George's enemies, had this become widely known.[15]

Yet the Bank's minutes tell it all. John Campbell would lift from his diary the substance of the entries for 1st to 3rd October and put them in the Bank's minute book; also the diary record of the further substantial demands in October made on the Royal Bank - and the ready assent by Campbell and his directors to these - up to the very day on which the Highland Army left Edinburgh for the invasion of England. The whole episode whereby from 3rd to 31st October the Royal Bank released large amounts of money for the Highland Army as it prepared to invade England remains a curious and perplexing aspect of the history of the Rising. Perhaps it had a sequel in the profound antipathy that the Duke of Cumberland developed towards Edinburgh. After Culloden it was at the Duke's insistence that 'disloyal' Edinburgh be punished by the ceremonial burning at the Mercat Cross in the High Street of rebel standards captured at the battle, and it was his recommendation to the King, his father, that Edinburgh should no longer be the capital of North Britain, that honour being transferred to reliable, whiggish Glasgow!

* * *

From mid October John Campbell's diary reverts to being a sort of register of his correspondence. To Lady Glenorchy in London he continues to send copies of the *Caledonian Mercury* (was she annoyed at its jubilant Jacobitism when she asked on 15th October that no more copies be sent?);

and he receives a flow of letters from her ladyship, for, throughout the
Jacobite occupation it is a remarkable fact that the mails to and from the
south still went through. To Lord Glenorchy, now endeavouring to take a
grip of the rebellion in Perthshire from Taymouth, he sends news and a
'half pound fine green tea'. He continues to keep in close touch with Lord
Monzie near Crieff, with Campbell of Auchalader, and with Campbell of St
Germains in East Lothian. The diary also continues to be an aide memoire
of all manner of transactions. A further visit (15 October) to Edinburgh
Castle, besieged no more, to see to Bank business in the vaults of the
Governor's House, which included the subventing of the garrison from the
Bank's funds and the burning of more notes already lodged there. He oversees
the welfare of the young daughter of Campbell of Inverawe (10th and 12th
October) stranded in Edinburgh and unable to get to her Argyllshire home.
He sends Campbell of Auchalader, 'who is a dying', freeze 'cloths' and
receives a new coat of his own from 'Niccol the taylor'.

The diary intersperses all this with comment on the events in town.
The continuing vigorous bombardment of Edinburgh by the guns of the
Castle's great Half-Moon battery on 4th and 5th October, which the citizens
were sure would lead to the total destruction of the tall lands of the
Lawnmarket and all down the High Street, is noted. However the
conclusion to the entry for 5th October reads 'Blocade taken off the Castle
this night by the Prince per printed notification to the inhabitants'.
And so the guns fell silent.

John Campbell had received calls from highland gentlemen who were
officer prisoners from Cope's army, taken at the battle of Prestonpans.
He had, however, friends in both camps. There continues to be a good deal
of evidence of friendly relationships with officers of the Highland Army.
A John Murray (not to be confused with John Murray of Broughton), who
was constantly, it seems, by the Earl of Breadalbane's side at Holyrood,
had no difficulty in securing from the Jacobite command protection for the
East Lothian property of Campbell of St Germains and passes for others at
John Campbell's instance. On the expedition to the Castle of 3rd October
Campbell had been entrusted with letters from General Guest, on behalf of
Cameron of Lochiel, about the imprisonment by the Fort William garrison
of Lochiel's brother, John Cameron of Fassifern, and he seeks Lochiel at
Mrs Clerk's tavern to pass on the general's response (8th October). Two

days later he learns of a French ship landed at Montrose. The following week he hears that 'one of distinction from thence lodges in Abbey' (i.e. Holyrood). This was the Marquis d'Eguilles, the observer sent in great secrecy from the Court of Louis XV, whose presence Charles Edward immediately turned to his own advantage by according him full ambassadorial honours as the harbinger (as the Prince would have it) of an early cross-Channel invasion by the army of France. Campbell, also on the 10th October, 'saw a letter of Lord Lovat's, about his Clan etc rising', which as matters stood must also have been highly confidential information.

An entry of particular interest is that for 26th October. 'Mungo Roro calld at me and breakfasted.... Mr Kinloch's servant maid came to acquaint me that her master's house at Bruntfield Links was robbd and pillaged last night by 15 highlanders and 2 women ... I beged of Mungo Roro to get all the information he could, and if possible to recover the goods that the rogues might be punished, which he undertook so far as lay in his power'. 'Mungo Roro' was Captain MacGregor of Roro of the Atholl Brigade; Roro far up Glenlyon where the men were 'out' in the Rising, and the thieves were probably some Clan Gregor desperadoes from the Perthshire hills. Would one be wrong in reading into this entry as great a concern for the good name of the Highland Army as for Mr Kinloch's property? 'Inshewen', who calls on Campbell as the Highland Army prepares to march south, is McNabb of Inishewan in Glen Lochay, an officer in the Duke of Perth's regiment. As Inishewan's purpose in making this call before he left for England with the Highland Army was to ask Campbell to send on his behalf a letter to Campbell of Auchalader, the factor for the Breadalbane Estate within which Inishewan lay, the complexity of relationships in this civil war is further illustrated.

The diary also meticulously records the further payments (already mentioned) made from the sacks of guineas which had been brought down from the Castle, as Royal Bank notes fell into Jacobite hands - £1,819 on 21st October, £1,117 on the 24th October and £400 on 26th October. Despite the reported reproof from Lord Milton, then at Berwick, three directors and the same number of extraordinary directors, marshalled by Campbell, on 28th October resolved 'in case any after demand should be made upon the bank by the Pr[ince] within £2,000, that the same should be answerd as formerly...'. This on the very eve of the march to England.

A final payment of £174 should have been made on lst November, the day on which the Highland Army left Edinburgh and took the roads to the south. But the 'protest' was wrongly dated, the handover should have taken place the day before, and the requisite 'notary and witnesses having left the town and Broughton was likewise gone' the payment could not be made.

Of John Campbell's inmost feelings, which must have been intense, the diary gives no indication. The rank and file of the Jacobite army were in good heart, but some of their leaders were dismayed at leaving Scotland. More clear-sighted than any, d'Eguilles, the French 'ambassador', saw that the army was doomed if there were to be no French invasion. 'However', he wrote in his despatch to Versailles, 'happily I can console myself by relying on their courage, their pride and the terror they inspire in their enemies'.[16]

The entry for lst November in this most laconic of diaries says simply 'Highland [Army] left this place wholly today' (and the following day Patrick Crichton, at nearby Woodhouselee, noted that the leaders of its western column 'had entertainment from Mrs Philp [wife of the Royal Bank director] at her house of Greenlaw'[17]). Twelve days later John Campbell noted in his diary that 'this day the judges enterd the City in procession', and so Lord Milton was able to resume his chairmanship of meetings of the Royal Bank's directors, which he duly did. The following day after going down to Holyrood in a chair to discuss matters with the Earl and returning by the same conveyance through 'a boisterous night' he notes that '2000 foot and dragoons enterd the City this evening'. Edinburgh's Jacobite interlude was at an end.

Before that, however, John Campbell had performed a signal service for Edinburgh. With the Highland Army gone, the fickle Edinburgh mob - another account blames the embittered soldiery of Lascelles' Regiment from the Castle's garrison - wasted no time in ransacking the Prince's apartment at Holyrood. The Earl of Breadalbane was alarmed; the vandals might not stop at the apartments on the first floor and were 'like to destroy the house and every thing in it'. The old Earl asked Campbell to persuade General Guest to put a stop to the havoc. Campbell acted promptly and the general, he learned, 'was immediatly to send down a Guard to the Abbey to protect it'. And so Holyrood was saved.

John Campbell was something of a poet. 'Poem' says the last word for his diary entry for 28th October. 'Poem continued', says the entry for the following day. 'Finished my composure' that for the 11th November. One wonders what had moved him to put his thoughts in verse at this juncture when the Highland Army had embarked on its 'noble attempt'?

Presumably this was Gaelic verse. It has not survived. What has survived is Gaelic verse by Duncan Bàn MacIntyre, celebrating the John Campbell of the Bank of later years. As a young man *Donnachadh Bàhn* had fought - if that is the word for it - in the ranks of the Argyll Regiment of Militia which broke and ran before the Jacobite onslaught at the Battle of Falkirk in the 'Forty-Five. However, he has in his poetry made it clear that his sympathies were entirely with the Prince's Cause. In 1766 he moved to Edinburgh from his post as a forester on the Breadalbane Estate; and it may have been after this that he wrote his poem *Song to John Campbell, Banker*. This is fulsome Gaelic praise poetry in which Campbell is addressed as if he were a highland warrior-chieftain of old. A verse is bestowed on the beauty of his horses and the elegance of his horsemanship; another lists lovingly his weaponry, targe, broadsword, pistols and musket; others on his admiration for pipe music, on the generous hospitality dispersed at Restalrig while 'candlesticks of silver/fierce blaze from the wax/throughout the whole mansion', and on the stateliness of his bearing as he welcomed friends, some the highest in the land (meaning, no doubt, the Duke of Argyll). The poem concludes with the lines:

> Glad tidings to cheer me would be
> If I were to see thee tomorrow
> Invested with the Crown,
> Amid rejoicing and pomp,
> Instead of King George.

A salutation from one former crypto-Jacobite to another?

* * *

In 1986 there came up for sale at Christie's a Jacobite wine-glass of the rare and once highly treasonable variety known as 'Amen' glass.[18] It had engraved on it a couple of verses of the Jacobite anthem 'God bless the king, I pray ....', which concluded with 'Amen'. That there be no doubt which king was intended, there was also a dedication to Charles Edward's brother, the Duke of York, and the figure '8' ,worked into the royal cipher. This last, meaning King James VIII of Scotland (and III of England), indicated its Scottish origin. It has been dated to between 1744 and 1746.

The provenance of this wine-glass leads back to a previous owner, the 2nd Marquess of Breadalbane, who lived at Taymouth Castle in the mid-nineteenth century. He is said to have been something of a collector, and a sentimental Jacobitism was in fashion. But the possibility cannot be discounted that the trail of ownership leads back to the aged 2nd Earl, his ancestor. To which King, one wonders, did the 2nd Earl of Breadalbane and his nephew John Campbell direct the loyal toast, when they dined together at Holyrood during the autumn of 1745?

References:

1. *Leaves from the Diary of an Edinburgh Banker in 1745* (Edinburgh, 1881). Reprinted in Scottish History Society, *Miscellany of the Scottish History Society* (Edinburgh, 1893)
2. Walter Biggar Blaikie, 'Edinburgh at the Time of the Occupation of Prince Charles', *Book of the Old Edinburgh Club 1909, vol.2* (Edinburgh, 1910), 1-60
3. Neil Munro, *The History of The Royal Bank of Scotland 1727-1927* (Edinburgh, 1928), 91-107
4. S G Checkland, *Scottish Banking, A History 1695-1973* (Glasgow, 1975), 71-4
5. A W Kerr, *History of Banking in Scotland* (4th edition, London, 1926), 59
6. J Macky, *Memoirs of the Secret Services of John Macky* (London, 1895), 199
7. Henrietta Tayler, ed., *The History of the Rebellion in the Years 1745 and 1746* (London, 1944), 9
8. Alexander Carlyle, *Anecdotes and Characters of the Times* (London, 1973), 69
9. A Francis Steuart, ed., *The Woodhouselee Manuscript: A Narrative of Events in Edinburgh and District During the Jacobite Occupation September to November 1745* (Edinburgh, 1907)
10. Henrietta Tayler, ed., ' Two Letters from Magdalen Pringle', *A Jacobite Miscellany* (London, 1948), 39
11. Leslie Stephen and Sidney Lee, ed., 'General Joshua Guest', *Dictionary of National Biography (London, 1890), 320*
12. John Home, *History of the Rebellion in the Year 1745* (Edinburgh, 1822), 92
13. Blaikie, op.cit., 47-8
14. Sir James Fergusson, *Argyll in the 'Forty-Five* (London, 1951), 255-56
15. Private communication to the author
16. G Lefèvre-Pontalis, *La Mission du Marquis d'Eguilles* (Paris, 1886)
17. Steuart, op. cit., 83
18. Geoffrey B Seddon, *The Jacobites and their Drinking Glasses* (Woodbridge, 1995), 188

Further reading:

Checkland, S G, *Scottish Banking, A History 1695-1973* (Glasgow, 1975)

Fergusson, Sir James, *Argyll in the 'Forty-Five* (London, 1951)

Gibson, John S, *Lochiel of the '45: The Jacobite Chief and the Prince* (Edinburgh, 1994)

Gibson, John S, *Bonnie Prince Charlie at Holyroodhouse: Edinburgh in the '45* (Edinburgh, forthcoming 1995)

Lenman, Bruce, *The Jacobite Risings in Britain (1689-1746)* (London, 1980; reprinted Aberdeen, 1995)

Maclean, Fitzroy, *Bonnie Prince Charlie* (London, 1988)

McLynn, Frank, *Charles Edward Stuart: A Tragedy in Many Acts* (London, 1988)

THE DIARY

Saturday 14 September 1745

On news of the highland army's approach, all the effects of the Bank were packt up, and partly transported to the C[astle] this night per memorandum apart. Lord G[lenorchy]'s boxes likewise transported. Paid sundrys to workmen for the Bank. Mind to answer William Mollison's letter of 11th per Aberdeen and Glenoure's of same date and Carwhin's of the 4th. Wrote to Lady Glenorchy.

Sunday 15th

The rest of the Bank effects transported to the C[astle]. Paid sundrys for the Bank workmen today. Received letter from Mr Mathias of the 10th. Received letter from Lord M[onzie] of the 15th. Received a l[   ].

Monday 16th September

Received a letter from Lord Justice Clerk desiring me to let him have £100. A highland gentleman of E[arl] Loudoun's regiment deliverd me this letter in the Castle of Edinburgh, on which I came down for my keys, met the Justice Clerk on the street, desired me to give the money to his Lady with whom he was to leave bank notes or draught on his cash account for the value, went back to the Castle took the money in half guineas out of my balance chest there and returnd to Edinburgh deliverd the £100 to Lady Milnton in her own house but got no value, nor have I seen the Justice Clerk since.

Highland army near Edinburgh per Courant. I dined with Coulterallers. Saw the Dragoons run off along the north side of Edinburgh. The town in a consternation all day. Volunteers arms deliverd in to the Castle on allarm of the firebell in the evening. Answered Messrs G[eorge] Middleton and Company's letter of the 12th. Wrote to Mr James Mathias about Eq[uivalen]t affairs. Wrote likewise to him about private occurrances. Deputation of the Magistracy sent out to Bellsmilns to capitulate with the P[rince] as to the surrender of the town, without effect.

Tuesday 17 September

Edinburgh taken by the highland army 1200 men sent in early in the morning. Numbers of highlanders crowd in to town all the day long. Sundry proclamations over the Cross. Prince enters Holyroodhouse. His army encamps in the King's Park. Answered Lord G[lenorchy]'s letter of the 11th from Ardmady. To answer Mr Robinson's letter of this date. Answered Messrs Middleton and Company's letter of the 12th. Answered Mr Mathias' letter of the 10th about Eq[uivalen]t Company. To answer Bank of England's letter of this date as well as their former with the b[il]l state[ment].

18th September

Mercury published an account of taking of Edinburgh - and proceedings of the army for some days preceeding. Wrote to Lord G[lenorchy] inclosed to Shereff Campbell. Wrote to Lady G[lenorchy]. Wrote to Mr Mathias.

Wednesday 18 September.

Wrote to Lord G[lenorchy] and sent it with my former letter designd to go under Shereff C[ampbell's] cover by Auchalader's servant.

Thursday 19 September

Highland army decampd from Dudingston late at night. Wrote to Lord Monzie per carrier. Wrote to Lord G[lenorchy] per ditto. Wrote to Lady G[lenorchy]. Wrote to Mr Mathias.

Friday 20th September

Highland army march towards Tranent and ly on their arms all night thereabouts. General Cope gets in to a fastness below and to the north of them towards the sea.

Saturday 21 September

Battle of Gladesmuir or Tranent fought wherin the highlanders routed General Cope.

| Notified per express*
 * Jock | } | to Lord Monzie
 Auchalader
 Lord Glenorchy |
| Ditto per post to | } | Lady Glenorchy
 Mr Mathias |

Wrote to P[eter] and J[ohn] Murdoch about Bank business. Had a letter from G[eorge] Innes calling me up to the Castle about sundrys and went, and gave out some money out of my balance per memorandums left in the chest. Drew for £90 on my cash account and took down the same in silver.

Sunday 22nd September

No sermon in the churches.

Monday 23 September

Mercury published giving an account of the battle and journal of the army from 27th August to this date. It likewise contains serious reflections theron.

Had a letter from G[eorge] Innes desiring to send up an iron keeper for the lock of his vault, which was got done. Directors proposd to burn notes in the C[astle] and sent me there to obtain access for them.

Tuesday 24 September

Courant published an imperfect account of the battle. Answered Lady G[lenorchy]'s letter of the 17th. Answered her letter of the 19th. Wrote to Mathias and sent the Mercury to all of them. A message from G[eorge] I[nnes] signifying the d[irectors] would have access to the Castle when they pleased, but they delayed cancelling the notes for some time.

Wednesday 25 September

Received £200 silver from A Brown's son. Answered Byers's letter per James Lyon <This letter returnd to me>, and sent him £7 in Old B[ank] notes which I received on his account from William Mackewan writer per bill on him to me per Byers, which was discharged. Despatched Dun[can] Campbell cousine to Auchlyne with letters to Lord G[lenorchy] with sundrys inclosed. Wrote then to Auchalader elder and younger and sent the Mercury about the battle to each of them. Also the Mercury of this date with further particulars of the battle. Earl [of] B[readalbane] drew on me to d[ebit] Dun[can] Cam[pbell] for a guinea which I paid him per receipt. Had a message from G[eorge] I[nnes] for money and went up to the Castle, saw him and his wife and did some business there. Had a letter from postmaster of Darlington that he had forwarded my letter to Lady G[lenorchy]. Mercury published containing 3 sundry proclamations by the Prince. <28 September deliverd to him this day> £3.12 lodgd with me by Ro[ber]t Barcaldines brought till his return from Moffat.

Thursday 26 September 1745

I was calld upon by Mr J[ohn] Philp to go to the Castle. Went with him. Saw General Guest. Gave General Guest £50 in half guineas out of my balance on Lord J[ustice] Clerk's draught which I lodged in chest in the Castle. Changed £5 note to Mr David Lyon in the Castle and gave him gold for same out of my balance having lodged that note in the chest. On my return from the Castle dind at home solus. Calld a meeting of directors at 3 a clock and Messrs Hamilton, Shairp and Philp met, and were of opinion they could not without a quorum order out the money wanted by G[eorge] I[nnes] and read and approvd of a letter I wrote to him to that effect. <Dated Ardmady 18th> Received a packet this morning from Lord G[lenorchy] per Anderson with a letter for my Lady which I forwarded this night. I wrote to her Ladyship and sent the Mercury of 25 instant and sent cook maid's account. I likewise got a letter for Lord C[hancello]r but did not send off as yet. Got a letter likewise from Lord M[onzie] dated 22 which I answerd this night per Crief post. Wrote to Mr Mathias and sent him Mercury of 25th instant. Got a letter from St G[ermans] by his servant telling of his bad usage by the highlanders. In consequence of which I wrote to Mr J[ohn] Murray at E[arl of] B[readalbane]'s to get a protection and pass. Received £200 in silver from A Brown, and gave his son receipt for this and as much received last night bearing yesterday's date, in all £400 for the Bank. To call at Mr J[ohn] M[urray] tomorrow's morning about

St G[erman]'s protection and pass. To answer Knockbuie's letter of 23rd which I received this day.

Friday 27th September

Went to the Abbey to see E[arl of] B[readalbane] who told me the Pr[ince] was visiting him last night. Saw Mr J[ohn] Murray who told me he would send up the protection for St Germans and pass, as soon as obtaind. Saw Mr Philp about cash for G[eorge] I[nnes] but he did not incline to grant warrant. Calld to see if Mr Coutts was come home to try if he would concurr but was not. Called at the Chancery, and got up E[arl of] Breadalbane's patent of honour which lay there to be recorded in terms of the Interlo[cuto]r of the Lords of Session, it having been neglected at passing the same in 1681. But delayed taking out the extract, and in case I was not to take it out at all, am to pay for the writing. Told Mr Philp that Provost Coutts was not come to town. Dined at home J C ... with me. Andrew Brown clerk of the mines calld upon me and gave me his joint bill with Lady Lombe for £30. She owd me (and discharged the old bill) payable in 6 months. Got a letter from G[eorge] Innes about cash, which I answered, desiring him to get as much as he wanted out of the tellers balances. Got a letter from Auch[ala]der desiring to get him a suit of cloaths which I bespoke at James Stirlings. Mercury published with a proclamation about the Banks, and rectifying some articles formerly published as to the battle, also publishing the Act of Regency and Manifesto. Saw Mr Trotter who told me he has Provost Coutts's bankkey. Got a protection for the estate, houses and effects of St G[ermans] and allowance for passing and repassing about his lawfull affairs, and gave Mr Murray's servant 2 shillings 6 pence. Bespoke a frize coat for my self at James Stirling's, and orderd Niccol to make it.

Saturday 28 September

Dispatched St G[erman]'s servant home with the protection. Sent to Mr Trotter for Provost Coutts' bankkey which I got seald. Advised Messrs Hamilton and Philp that I had got the key, and they have appointed $^1/2$ past ten to go to the Castle to settle with G[eorge] Innes. I sent to the accomptant and tellers to attend. We all went up to the Castle gate, but could not get access. G[eorge] I[nnes] was insulted by the officer of the guard. Wrote to Auchalader telling I had bespoke his cloths and sent him last Mercury by the man who came in with the clerk's son, and sent him at the same time a pound Bohea tea at 9 shillings from James Stirling's. Took leave of Captain McNab, he being to sett out by 6 next morning to Perth with the rest of the officers who are prisoners. Wrote to Lady G[lenorchy] and sent her Mercury of the 27 and one from E[arl of] B[readalbane]. Wrote to Mr Mathias and sent him Mercury of 27th. Wrote to Lord M[onzie] ditto. Wrote to Carwhin. Took leave of Ensign Allan Campbell prisoner.

Sunday 29 September

No sermon in churches. Dined at home D[avid] B[aillie] with me. Mr James Veitch calld upon us and went together to John's coffee house. In the evening G[eorge] Innes calld upon me, he having come down from the Castle the night before.

Monday 30 September

The London post due yesterday came in this morning by which I received: Letter from Lady G[lenorchy] dated Tuesday 25 should be 24. Letter from Captain Stirling dated Plymouth 20th and inclosed letter from Jo[hn] Graham surgeon dated on board Spence sloop Lagos Bay 27 July 1745 and with it received further, letter of attorney from ditto J[ohn] Graham dated 27 July at sea there no stampt paper was to be had.

Mr John Philp calld on me to whom I lent £8 on his notes, whereof £5 in silver out of the £90 bag I took out of my balance in the Castle, and £3 in 20 shilling notes. Had a message from E[arl of] B[readalbane] to dine with him, but can't comply because of the consternation the town is in, the Castle having threatned to fire if the highland guard at the weighhouse was not removd. Took £10 for my own use out of the £90 silver bag, so that there now only remains £75. Got home 6 new shirts and paid Marg[are]t Jack for cambrick and making £1.10 whereof £1 formerly lodged with Betty for buying the cambrick. Inhabitants met in new church to consult on a letter they had received from General Guest threatning that unless the communication between the City and Castle was opened they would fire upon the City. Deputies thereupon sent from the City of Edinb[urgh] to the Prince with General Guest's letter. To which the P[rince] gave an answer which is now printed. On this answer hostilities from the Castle suspended for 6 days. Numbers of the inhabitants movd their families and effects out of town all this day. The City being somewhat calmed about 1 a clock I went down to the Abbey where all was quiet, dined with E[arl of] B[readalbane] and Mr Murray. Returned at 3 in a chair, came home. Went to the coffee house, there staid till the evening that I came home for all the night. Sent messages to Lord Mon[zie] and Lord Tinw[ald]'s servants to pacify them as to their fears and to se[ver]al other families of my acquaintance.

Tuesday 1 October 1745

Wrote to Captain J[ohn] Stirling in answer to his from Plymouth of 20 September and sent him a letter inclosed from his wife. This letter I addresst to Forrest's coffee house near Charring Cross. Had a verbal message from Provost Coutts now at Allanbank per his friend Mr Coutts about Bank affairs. Dind with Messrs Veitch and Baillie at Turnbull's. Wrote to G[eorge] S[tirling] younger of Auchyll Place Herbertshire per Falkirk post <This went by Herbert carrier> to notify his father's arrival at Plymouth. Received letter from Pendrich which I answered about the renewal of his bill to the Bank, and advised him of Captain Stirling's arrival in England. Between 6 and 7 a clock at night a protest was then taken against me as Cashier of the R[oyal] Bank by John Murray of Broughton esquire as Secretary to the Prince for payment of £857 Royal Bank notes, (which he exhibited) in the current coin of the kingdom, and on failzure thereof within 48 hours, that the estates and effects of the directors and managers should be distressed for the same. I answered that by reason of the commotions in the countrey, the effects of the Bank were lately carried up to the Castle, for the security of all concerned, for as the directors acted, in a manner as factors for their constituents the proprietors it was judged reasonable, and what every body in their circumstances had done, to secure the effects of the company, that none might be sufferers in the issue: and matters were in that situation at present that there was no access to the Castle at any rate, for that Mr Jo[hn] Hamilton and Mr John Philp two of the directors had essayed to get in on Saturday last, with the accomptant and tellers and myself in order to do business, but that access was refused, though they continued at the gate for about an hour.

Duplyed by Mr Murray that he would in name of the Prince grant a pass and protection for <u>going to the gate</u>, and that he hoped the Governor woud give admittance, but whether he did or not, if the payment was not made, the order should be put in execution, after elapse of the time limited. And thereupon took instruments in the hands of William McKewan notary publick in presence of Mr Peter Smith, brother to deceast David Smith of Methven and Purves writer to the Signet, and thereafter a schedule of the protest was sent to me by Mr McKewan the notary, but not signed. Immediatly on Mr Murray's taking the above protest I waited upon Mr Jo[hn] Hamilton and Mr Philp the only two directors in town at Mrs Clerk's vintner, there shewd them the schedule, and what I have before here marked down, and after reasoning thereon agreed to try to get in to the Castle to morrow, and orderd Mr Shairp the only other director about the town to be summond for that purpose, to meet with them at my house by 9 in the morning, that this affair might be futher concerted, and if possible money might be got out for answering the demand, and to prepare the way to the gate, a pass and protection was to be obtained from the Prince, or from Mr Murray as Secretary for the directors and officers of the Bank to go that length to try if the Governor would give admittance.

Mean time that a letter be prepared to be sent to General Guest for notification, and <to prevent all mistake> to be first transmitted to Mr Murray for his perusall and, another to the absent directors to acquaint them with this event that the directors present might be justified at the hands of their constituents. Wrote to Lady G[lenorchy] and sent her the Courant of this date, containing copy letters to the Royal Burrows. To collectors of the land tax of all the shires in Scotland, and to the collectors and comptrollers of the customs and the Prince's answer to the deputation from City of Edinburgh about the message from the Castle that unless the communication with the town was opend they would fire upon it. Wrote to Lord G[lenorchy] per Anderson, by way of Monzie, and sent this day's Courant inclosed. Wrote then per ditto to Lord Monzie. Wrote to Jeanie Stirling at Herbert[shire] telling of her father's arrivall. Wrote to Mrs Stirling the same and to Dr Stirling per cover to hers. Wrote to Miss K C telling I woud write to her sister Mrs Menzies that all were well at M.

Wednesday 2nd October

Messrs Hamilton, Shairp and Philp met at my house at 9 a clock agreable to
appointment. Read over the letters prepared to be sent to General Guest and
Mr Murray. Indicted a meeting of ordinary and extraordinary directors to meet at
my house at 12 a clock for which purpose I made up and signd printed notes for
    Mr [Hugh] Hathorn and Mr William Forbes
    Mr William Grant
    Baillie [James] Mansfield
    and Mr [William] Keir
All of which notes were executed by Peter Campbell officer who reported that only
the first two were in town and they came and when present with the above three
ordinary directors they all agreed to the measure proposd. Accordingly Mr Da[vid]
Baillie was sent to the Abbey with these two letters which I signd and seald, and
these he deliverd to Mr Murray, who returned General Guest's letter and added
that there was to be a further demand upon the Bank, the particulars whereof he
would acquaint me of, as soon as possible. The directors adjourned to dine at Mrs
Clerk's to consider further of these affairs. But first read and approved of the
draught of a letter to be dispatched to the absent directors to notify these resolutions
to them.
    <2 a clock> Dispatched Ja[mes] Lyon porter, to the Castle with my letter to
General Guest under safeguard from Lochiel per white flagg. Had a letter from
St Germans which I answered thanking him for his kind invitation to me to go to
this house to shun the calamity threatened against the City of Edinburgh from the
Castle. Sent Lady Dunstaffnage by her boy 20 shillings in silver and thanked her
for her kind invitation to stay at her house during these troubles. While at dinner
at Mrs Clerk's about 3 a clock afternoon, Mr Peter Smith, brother to Methven,
calld me to another room and notified to me as Cashier that the Prince had a
further demand of current specie from the R[oyal] Bank for the sum of £2,307
sterling of their notes which he as attorney for his highness required payment of,
within 48 hours under the penaltys containd in Mr Murray of Broughton's former
protest of yesterdays date and exhibited the bank notes, in presence of William
Mackewan notary publick before these witnesses [ ] writer to the Signet and [ ].
This further demand I immediatly notified to the directors present in the next room
vizt Messrs Hamilton, Shairp, Philp, Hathorn and Forbes. After reasoning some
time thereon, they agreed to comply with this demand, as well as the former if
access could be got to the Castle.
    Some time after this, Ja[mes] Lyon the porter returned, and brought back the
letter for General Guest open, his excellency having read the same, but did not
incline to give a written answer, not having a lawyer to advise with, but added that
if the directors had come in a private manner, they might dispose of their own as
they won[te]d. After talking over this matter a little Mr Peter Smith calld me again,
and presented a pass to the Castle for the three ordinary directors and my self,
which pass was only to last and continue to this night at ten a clock. I expostulated
with him upon the impossibility of the thing, but he said that all excuse was in vain,

for that a gentleman, who understood the business of banking, was with the Prince, when the pass was a granting, who said that there was no difficulty in the thing, for that all the gold and silver must be in baggs of certain sums, and therefore that it was an easy matter, and required no great time to execute this affair, and so the Prince was positive to grant no longer indulgence. Hereupon Mr Smith left me and I returned to the directors and reported what past and being now towards evening, they found the measure proposd by the pass impracticable, so adjourned to my house to drink coffee and further to deliberate of the affair.

Bespoke a pott of coffee at Muirhead's. The directors talked over this exigency fully, and then resolved that a letter should be written by me to Mr Murray of Broughton desiring there the pass should be renewd for to morrow when they would try to get access to the Castle and bring down the cash, and that the new pass should comprehend not only the three ordinary directors contain'd in the former, vizt Messrs Hamilton, Shairp and Philp and my self, but likewise William Mitchell accomptant and Alexander Innes teller. Accordingly I wrote a letter in these terms which was read to and approvd of by the meeting, and being copied over fair by David Baillie, (who had formerly transcribed the other letters to General Guest and Mr Murray of Broughton in the forenoon) the same was signed by me as the other letters were in presence of, and by appointment of the meeting. On this the directors dismissed, and twas resolved that the three ordinary directors accomptant and A[lexander] Innes teller should meet at my house tomorrow between 8 and 9 in the morning. But before the meeting was over, A[lexander] Innes teller was calld upon, to know if his brother George was in the Castle, who told he was not, on which he was dispatched to his house, to know if he had lodged the keys of the Castle vault, where the Bank repositories were lodged, with his wife, and if he had, to bring them, which accordingly he deliverd to me in a seald parcell, which I opened, in presence of the directors, and then kept the keys, George Innes having gone in to the countrey some days agoe, as his wife told his brother.

Mr David Baillie got the charge of delivering the letter to Mr Murray of Broughton, after sealing, but after all search for him, he could not be found in town or Abbey on which Mr Baillie and I concerted, that I should call for Lochiel in Mrs Clerk's and tell him of the case, who brought me Mr Smith who, with others, were in company with him, and in Lochiel's presence I deliverd the letter to Mr Smith, who took burden to get and send me the answer this night, I then parted with these two gentlemen. All this discourse with them having past in the passage to Mrs Clerk's great room, and afterwards I went to John's coffee house where David Baillie waited me, to whom I told all that past. And then came home between 7 and 8 a clock.

A little before parting with the directors I received a large packet from Lord Glenorchy per Jock, dated from Taymouth 29 September, with letters inclosed for

Lady Glenorchy	
Lady Harriot C[ockburn]	All to be dispatched by
Philip Yorke esquire	tomorrow's post

I likewise received letter from Lord Monzie of the 29th September from Taymouth. Also a letter from Auchalader same date from Taymouth.

And one from his son John ditto. All to be answered. Baillie Wilson deliverd me a receipt by William Grant for 43,000 Easdale sclate for the use of John Robinson esquire dated at Buchlonhall 27 September 1745 which I'm to advise Carwhin of. Carwhin's bill on me to Provost Fisher for £37 dated 7 September at 8 days date was pro[tes]t by George Chalmer merchant in Leith, he having refused payment some days agoe in bank notes of any kind. Between 10 and 11 at night a servant came to me with the pass to and from the Castle, which is limited between 8 in the morning and 3 afternoon to morrow.

Thursday 3rd October 1745

About 7 this morning I wrote a letter to General Guest in the Castle acquainting him that Messrs John Hamilton, Alexander Shairp and John Philp directors of the R[oyal] Bank, William Mitchel accomptant, A[lexander] Innes teller and my self as Cashier intended to go up to the Castle upon Bank business, therefore that he would please to give the proper orders to the Captain of the Guard to give us admittance upon our displaying a white flagg. This letter I sent up with Ja[mes] Lyon porter, who used likewise a white napkin for his signall and he reported we should be admitted. About 8 a clock the five gentlemen above named met at my house, and after breakfast we proceeded on our expedition. This side of the weigh house I calld for the Captain of the highland guard (one Mr Cameron) to whom I shewd our pass, and after his reading the same, he calld for one of his men to go through all the centinells posted between that and the reservoir to give them due notice, and after waiting about a quarter of an hour, the Captain desired us to proceed, for that all was safe before us, he kept the pass in his custody to be deliverd to the next Captain when he was relieved off guard, I then hoisted my white flag and usherd the rest of the gentlemen saluting the centinells with it as we past, and as we approachd the Castle gate waved it often, at last the centinells there calld to us to come forward, and on our arrival at the bridge, telling who we were, 'twas lett down, the Captain received us in, between the bridge and the gate where he compard our names with my letter to General Guest which he had in his hand.

On our arrival at General Guest's lodgings, (which is the Governor's new house) the directors and I went in, told him our errand in general was to get in to the R[oyal] Bank repositories to do some business, and General Preston having come in at that instant, he was likewise told the same. After some short conversation we left the two generalls and proceeded to the place where all the Bank things are lodged, and executed the affairs we came about, according to particular memorandums and minutes thereof apart.

During our continuance in the Castle which was from about 9 'till near three a clock, there was closs firing from thence upon the Gardner's house at Livingston's yeards, occupied by R Taylor the shoemaker, at the head of a party of volunteers for the Prince, to stop the communication thereabouts with the Castle, and one Watson a soldier was so couragious as to go down over the Castle wall upon a rope, fire upon the Gardners house, kill some of the volunteers there, carried off a firelock or two from them, sett the house in fire, returned with these firelocks by his rope into the Castle, where he was received with loud huzzars for his valour. On his return the garrison was preparing for a sally, but as the men were a drawing up we got liberty from General Guest to go out again and Captain Robert Mirry escorted us to the gate, where I again raised my white flagg, and with my friends returned to town in safety, landed at my house from whence we adjournd to dine at Mrs Clerk's vintner.

No sooner were we sett down in Mrs Clerk's than we were informed that upon the sally from the Castle, Taylor and some of his men were taken and carried thither prisoners, leaving others dead on the spott, their house being sett on fire, the rest of the party having made their escape. Before I went to dinner I waited upon Mr John Murray of Broughton esquire and told him I was come from the directors to acquaint him that they were ready to exchange current coin for their notes, in terms and in consequence of the two sealed demands made upon the Bank by way of protests and certification. On which he appointed six a clock at night to receive the money at my house, which I reported to the directors in Mrs Clerk's, and after dinner I came down to make all ready and to keep the appointment having packd up the gold in baggs to the net amount of the demands being £3164. About 7 a clock in place of Mr Murrays coming himself, he sent one Mr Andrew Lumisdean (son to William Lumisdean writer in Edinburgh) his deputy secretary, who had with him the bank notes. I told him the money was ready on the table, but that I hoped he had the two protests duely discharged. He told me he had not, that they were of no moment, as they were never extended, on this we sent for William Mckewan the notary, who acknowleged they were not drawn up, but though they were 'twas to Mr Murray and not to me he was to deliver them, nor would Mr Lumisdean promise to get them discharged, not knowing Mr Murray's mind on that head. Being difficulted in this particular, and having no directors at hand to advise with, it was agreed and Mr Mckewan promised faithfully to make out the protests against to morrow's morning to be deliverd to Mr Murray, in case he should think proper to deliver them to the Bank.

Hereupon I calld up A[lexander] Innes teller, to compt over the notes, and that being done, the gold was likewise told over, first by Mr Innes, then by Mr Mackewan and last of all by Mr Lumisdean who put it up in sealed baggs, and these again in one large bag seald which he caused carry up to his chair. And so we parted about eleven a clock at night; having drunk one bottle of wine during our business. Thereafter I lodged notes in their proper place in Bank. The net sum paid was £3076, Mr Lumsdean having disposed of £88 of the notes some other way. The Castle continued firing on the highland guards at the weigh house. When in the Castle today I deliverd two letters to General Guest the charge of which I had from John McFarlane Writer to the Signet. Wrote to Lady Glenorchy and sent letters from Lord G[lenorchy] for her Ladyship, Lady Harriot C[ockburn] and Mr Yorke.

Friday 4th October 1745

Coulterallers calld upon me for a loan which I gave him per cash book. £5.
Mr Alexander Shairp calld upon me with a letter from Mr McCulloch to the

overseers of the linnen manufactory signifying the distress the work people were in
for want of silver coin, and desired I might assist him. Had a letter from Jeanie
Stirling inviting me to Herbert[shire] which I answerd by the gardner. John
Thomson calld at me to tell that Lord Tinwald was well.

After dinner Mr Shairp,		all calld for silver coin the first four
Mr McCulloch,		in exchange for notes and E[arl of]
D Hathorn,		B[readalbane]'s servant per
Mr Jo[hn]		his Lordship's receipt which I
Hamilton's servant,	}	answerd in all 59 out of a bag
E[arl of]		of A Brown's and sent Auchalader
B[readalbane]'s		20 shillings out of it and £4 out
servant, Finlay		of my own Castle bag.

Wrote to Lord Glenorchy in answer to his of 29 September and sent him 3 Mercurys
vizt 30 September, 2 and 4 October and $1/2$ pound fine green tea. Wrote to Lord
Monzie and sent him ditto. Wrote to Auchalader and sent him ditto and £5 silver.
Wrote to young Auchalader and sent 3 Mercurys. All these per McGrigor workman
at Taymouth. As my letters were ready for sealing and to be despatched per Jock,
the forsaid McGrigor came in with letters from Lord G[lenorchy] and Auchalader
of the 2nd which I likewise answerd, and my letters lying now seald, the man is to
call at me when he gets a pass from Lochiel in the morning. In this last letter of
Lord Glenorchy's he desires me to make out proxies for E[arl of] B[readalbane] to
sign and to be sent to Lady G[lenorchy] at London.

The Castle has continued firing most of this day and night on some of the
uppermost houses on the Castlehill, where the highland Guards shelterd themselves,
fired one of them, and some people killed near the weigh house. Had a message
from J[ohn] G[raham] secretary by his servant who left him at Alnwick, desiring
me to look at some papers his servant was to get in his scritore and to be sent to
him. He accordingly brought the papers, but without inspection I seald them up
with his and my own seal to ly at my house till further orders least they might be
taken from the servant on the road, as he was robbd in the incoming, and wrote to
Mr Graham accordingly, and desired him to send directions about his furniture etc
as James's Court where he lives is much exposed to the firing of the Castle.

Saturday 5th October 1745

Wrote two copies of proxies by E[arl of] B[readalbane] to Lord Chancellor on
parchment. Went down and dined at the Abbey and got them signed and sealed.
Waited upon Mr Murray of Broughton desired from him the protests taken by him
against the R[oyal] B[ank] he scroupled as he saw no occasion for them, I added as
one prin[cipa]l reason for my asking them was that the repositories were broke
open when there was not a court of directors present, therefore in justification of
all concerned 'twas necessary to have them. He then gave his deputy Mr Lumsdean
orders to cause the notary extend them, and on my return to town I sent Mr
Mackewan a message to that purpose. Dispatched the Earl's proxy which was seald

up in a letter to the Lord Chancellor, and that again in a letter which I wrote to Lady Glenorchy therein I likewise sent her the Mercury of the 4th instant. Niccol the taylor brought me my freese coat, and I paid his account. The other proxy which lys by me executed to be sent off by some private hand going to London in case this should miscarry. Answerd a letter of St German's this forenoon. Constant fireing from the Castle. Blocade taken off the Castle this night by the Prince per printed notification to the inhabitants.

Sunday 6 October 1745

No sermon in the churches. Sent the E[arl] of Breadalbane the key of his little cabinet which lay by me seald since he fell ill, I say sent it seald to his Lordship by my servant Allick. I was not abroad all this day.

Monday 7th October

Mrs Kinloch lodged £37 in R[oyal] B[ank] notes with me for which I deliverd a promissary note to her to be deliverd to her husband. Saw William Mackewan the notary who shewd me the Bank protests extended and signd only he wanted one of the witnesses, whom he was to get and then to send down the protests to the Secretary's office. The E[arl] of B[readalbane] having dispatched Jock to Lord M[onzie] I wrote by him to Lord Monzie, and to Lord Glenorchy and sent each a copy of susp[ension] of the Castle blocade. I then wrote likewise to Auchalader telling I could not get his cloaths out of his taylor's hands. Had a visit from Mr William Monro. Paid Murray and Company of arrears of maggazine due by Carwhin per receipt being 9 shillings in Mr Sanders's time. Paid Jock 10 shillings which with 6 shillings formerly is in full for going last time to Breadalbane having gone the length of Tymdrom and on his return 8 miles above Stirling besides freighting a yole in going and got nothing while he continued in the countrey. Busy making up Bank minutes since 14 instant.

Tuesday 8 October

Calld for Lochiel about the letters deliverd me by Mr John McFarlane to General Guest, about Fassiefern's imprisonment at Fort William, but missed Lochiel. Went to the coffee house and read the news. On my way home met the accomptant and Robert Selkrig teller, who came alongs, and I got the latter to sort all the R[oyal] B[ank] notes I had got from Mr Lumisdean in order to be ready for cancelling, and that being done lodged these notes back in their proper place. Dined at home s[olus]. Had a message from L[ochiel] about the letters to General Guest but could give him no answer other than that I deliverd them to the General as directed. Evening spent in making further progress in my minutes of Bank affairs. Had a letter from St G[ermans] this forenoon, which I answered. Wrote to Lady G[lenorchy] and sent her the news paper, I mean the Mercury of yesterday's date. Sent a message to Mr Lumisdean per P Croster about Bank protests, but they were not then come to his hand.

Wednesday 9 October 1745

Waited upon Provost Coutts at his own house this morning, having sent me a message he was come to town. Went to John's coffeehouse. Sent for William McKewan notary about Bank protests. On his coming, shewd me the protests duely signed, and inclosed them in a letter which was sent by my servant Allick to Mr Andrew Lumisdean at the Abbey, who promised to return them to me discharged very soon. Came home before dinner, and was calld upon by a servant of Sir Charles G[ilmore]'s with whom I went to Pleasants and got two letters from Lady G[lenorchy]. Dined at home s[olus]. Had a visit from A B merchant about his advertisement. Had a visit from Baillie Mansfield. D[avid] Baillie calld upon me to tell he had sent Ja[mes] Lyon porter to Mr Shairp that he might sign the Bank establishment. Lyon brought the establishment, and I paid D[avid] B[aillie] his £10 per receipt thereon. To get the initials of 2 directors to the inventory of parcel of £5 notes cancelld in the Castle being £5600 as marked by Mr Shairp's hand in the inventary. And likewise to another parcell of £6700 also marked by Mr Shairp as cancelld. And likewise to the inventory of large unfinished books of R[oyal] Bank notes cancelld, this last being only marked by Mr Hamilton as yet. Lord Monzie's house maid calld at me for money to maintain her, and I gave her 10 shillings. Busy making up Bank minutes. <Countermanded> Know whether to despatch letters to absent directors about the demand made. <10 October done this day per Sir C[harles] G[ilmore]'s servant> Send off letter to Chancellor also proxy.

Thursday 10th October 1745

Went to the coffee house. On my return, saw Mr Shairp, who came home with me, and read over all the Bank minutes which I made out from 14 September, and put his initials to two parcells of notes cancelld in the Castle which he had formerly with his own hand markd down. George Gordon calld upon me and told of the French ship landed at Montrose. Saw a letter of Lord Lovat's, about his Clan etc rising. Went to the Abbey and calld at Mr Lumisdean for the two protests against the R[oyal] Bank who promised to send them to me to E[arl of] Breadalbane's. Dined with E[arl of] B[readalbane], Miss Boswell, Peggy Skene and J[ohn] Murray. After dinner sent to Mr Lumisdean for the Bank protests, which he sent me discharged. E[arl of] B[readalbane] gave me a letter and pass for his son to go to England also a pass to John McDiarmid to be sent with these to Taymouth. On my return to town got a letter from Lady G[lenorchy] 5 instant per post which was opened, but not the one for Lord G[lenorchy] which was inclosd. Answered that letter of her Ladyship's per Sir Charles Gilmore's servant who was going the length of Alnwick, to whom I gave half a crown for care (besides 2 shillings when he brought me the letter yesterday) and in that letter for my lady I inclosd one for Lord Ch[ancello]r from Lord G[lenorchy] which had lyen by me for some time and likewise the 2nd copy of the E[arl']s proxy to Lord Ch[ancello]r in case the former sent by post had miscarried. Also Mercury of the 9th.

I then despatched John McDiarmid, and sent by him to Lord G[lenorchy] 3 letters from my Lady. The Earl's letters and pass, and a long letter from my self and one from J[ohn] Murray. Sent by him likewise a letter for Lord G[lenorchy] covering the news papers, I mean the Mercury of the 9th. Sent likewise by him letter to Lord M[onzie] to the care of Lieutenant James Campbell in the Castle of Stirling, answering his Lordship's of the 7th and 9th and sent him Mercury of the 9th about Glenco and discharging any members to go Parliament. Wrote to Dr Stirling to take care of the letter for Lord Monzie, and to protect McDiarmid if necessary. I kept a copy of the pass to Lord G[lenorchy] and advised Lord M[onzie] of that whole affair fully. Wrote to Lady G[lenorchy] per post, advising that I had written to her this night by Sir Charles Gilmor[e] or Sir Jo[hn] Inglis's servant and that by him I had sent the proxy and letter to Lord C[hancello]r. Got a letter from Lady Inveraw with one inclosed to Miss Jessie Campbell, went to see her daughter at Mrs C's but the family was gone to Dalkeith. <done>To answer this letter.

Friday 11th October 1745

Barclay the taylor brought me home Auchalader's cloaths. I paid Carwhin's draght on me £37 to the order of Provost Fisher. Had a letter from Lord Monzie on Jock's return, dated yesterdays morning. Jock advised me he had left my letters for Lord Glen[orchy] at Monzie. Got A[lexander] Innes younger to tell over all my balances in iron chest.

Saturday 12 October

Changed £15 notes to Mr McCulloch and gave him a bag of shillings of £10 and a bag of 6 pence of £5 for the same. Changed £11 notes to Mr Shairp, and gave him half guineas and cash in silver for the same. <Messrs Hamilton, Coutts, Shairp> Read over the Bank minutes, present as per margin and asome ammendments all to sign them on Monday. Appointed Monday at 9 a clock to cancell notes. Orderd to pay £8.2.6 for contribution on the Bank house rent. Had a letter from Lord Glen[orchy] by McGrigor dated at Taymouth 9 October with one for my Lady. Wrote to Lady Glen[orchy] and sent her the letter from her Lord, and sent her Mercury of 9 and 11. That of the 9th formerly sent by Sir Jo[hn] Inglis' man not being yet gone off. Sent likewise to her Ladyship the Prince's declaration of the 10th addresst to all his father's subjects. Directors met at my house read over all the Bank minutes since 14 September as I have already mentioned. They are to meet again Monday's morning on Bank business. Had a letter from Lord Monzie of the 11th from Stirling per McGrigor with one inclosed for Mr Lundie which I'm to deliver to Coulterallers to send off. Had a letter from Auchalader about his son Peter. Send Lord G[lenorchy] £5 in silver. Wrote to Lady Inveraw that her daughter was well. Wrote to Carwhin and sent him Prince's declaration.

Sunday 13th October

No sermon in churches. Dined with E[arl of] B[readalbane] Taymouth and Mr J[ohn] M[urray]. Came home in the evening.

Monday 14th October 1745

A meeting of directors. Present Messrs Shairp, Coutts and Hamilton.
Cancelld parcells of notes vizt.

What I received from Broughton	3076
What received from General Guest part of my balance . . .	600
	3676
More part of ditto 20 shilling notes	1800

Calld a meeting of directors ordinary and extraordinary. Present Messrs Hamilton,
Shairp, Coutts, Hathorn, Forbes and Mansfield. Dined at Mrs Clerk's and talkd
over sundry bank business. Message per B[aillie] Mansfield to General Guest for
admittance about Bank business to the Castle agreed to. Meeting indicted for 9 to
morrow. Officers of the Bank came to me and I notified same. Had 1 b[ottle] of
wine. Supped at Mr Ron[al]d Craufurd's with sundrys.

Tuesday 15th October 1745

Coulterallers calld for loan of 6 guineas which I gave him on bill. Went to the Castle
with Provost Coutts, Da[vid] Baillie accomptant and his clerk Ewart and three
tellers about Bank business, having notified our intention to General Guest, by a
letter which I wrote to him per Baillie Mansfield. Before we went up had another
crave for half crown contribution on Bank house amounting to £8.2.6 which the
directors agreed to pay, so Baillie Mansfield was to advance it in my absence, and I
to repay him. Provost Coutts and I waited upon Generalls Guest and Preston in the
Castle. Then enterd upon our business in the vault vizt. Settled and balancd the
state of the cash since 11 September. I got payment of £440 from A[lexander] Innes'
servant which I had advancd on cash draughts and for which he now got credite.
Deliverd establishment of Bank sallurys to Robert Selkrig that he might pay and
state the same, he having paid me for my self £20 and for Mr Whitefoord £25. To
J[ohn] Graham and D[avid] Baillie £32.10. I gave ob[ligation] for Mr Whitefoords
and John Graham's part to procure their receipts being for £47:10. Alexander
Innes senior gave me receipt in my book with the tellers for £2000, and in discharge
of it he got credite for the like sum paid by me at the directors desire for
Mr Whitefoord to gen[era]l per receipt which receipts Mr Innes returnd me on my
ob[ligation]. All the Bank notes cancelled, whether taken from bank or out of my
balances this day stated to account. The tellers orderd to take down from the Castle
all their balances to be deliverd over to me, and likewise their telling book to
ascertain the same. My compt book with the tellers also taken down to ly by me. All
the notes formerly torn and not burnt, but laid up in the directors old chest under
lock, were this day burnt. All the bills on 60 days, not formerly brought down, were
deliverd to Da[vid] Baillie, his receipt or the Secretarys having formerly stood for
the same. All the forreign bills, and those from P[eter] Murdoch and Company
taken down by Robert Selkrig, in order to be lookt into. Vouchers of the cashier's
account with the directors from 11 September to this day, seald up by Mr Coutts
and lodged in my hands. All the books that were this day taken out of the boxes

for ballancing the cash, lodged in the directors' old chest the key whereof lodged
with me. Directors keys seald up by Mr Coutts lodged with me, also the bank seal
likewise seald up by him. Keys of the vault lodged with me but to be returnd to
Mrs Innes. On our coming from the Castle dined with Mr Coutts, D[avid] Baillie
and George Chalmers at lucky Clerks, paid bill 7 shillings. Went after dinner to
the Castle with Mr Coutts and D[avid] Baillie and saw all the business finished.
Came home, Provost Coutts and D[avid] Baillie with me, where the keys, seal,
and vouchers were seald up, as above mentioned, with Mr Coutts's seall. Answered
Lady Glen[orchy's] letters of 8 and 10 but sent her nothing inclosed, she having for-
bid to send any more news papers. Answered three letters of Lord Monzie's, but
missed the Stirling post. Got a letter from Dun[can] Cam[pbell]. Answered letter of
Lady Dunstaffnage's and sent her a guinea by her servant inclosed.

Wednesday 16 October 1745

Tellers
D[uncan] Cam[pbell]'s wife } calld at my house.
Mr Shairp

Went to the coffee house. Dined s[olus]. William Dow deliverd me a letter from
Lady G[lenorchy] dated 8 and another for Lord G[lenorchy] both per express, but
had been stopt on the road. A[lexander] Innes senior and junior ballan[ce]d their
cash. Robert Barcaldine's brother calld in the evening by whom I sent the letter I
wrote last night for Lord M[onzie] and enclosed the Mercurys of 14 and 16.
Answered St Germans' letter of this date.

Thursday 17 October

Tellers came to finish their balances. William Hogg's clerk calld for £40 in gold for
notes. Had a letter from Lady G[lenorchy] of the 12 acknowleging mine of the 5th
with what inclosed. Had a letter from Captain J[ohn] Stirling of the 12th. To
Captain Stirling's letter was annexed one for his wife, which I'm to send off. Dined
s[olus]. Went to the coffee house. Went through my balance. Wrote to Lord
G[lenorchy] per McGrigor and sent him one English letter (I know not from whom)
and £5 in silver. Sent him Mercurys of 11, 14 and 16. Sent Auchalader Mercurys of
9 and 11, 14 and 16. Sent him his new freese cloaths. Wrote to young Auchalader
and sent him the Mercurys of the 11, 14 and 16. Answerd Lady G[lenorchy]'s of the
8th and 12 told her all was well, quiet here, frequent reinforcements, ship landed at
Montrose, one of distinction from thence lodges in Abbey. Answerd Captain John
Stirling's letter of the 12 per Forrests coffee house. Wrote to George Stirling and
inclosed his father's letter to me per Falkirk post it having annexd to it a letter for
his mother from the Captain. Wrote to Lord Monzie. Settled sundrys of my bank
affairs by adjustments and cheques and found all to agree.

Friday 18 October 1745

Dispatched McGrigor this morning with all the letters which I wrote and seald last night and gave him 3s 6d. Had a letter from Byers which I answered. Had a letter from E[arl of] B[readalbane] which I answerd. Robert Selkrig came to sort notes, which he finished. Messrs Hamilton and Coutts mett and cancelld the same per signd inventary agreable to which I'm to have credite in part of my balances, amounting to £6539. They afterwards came down to my house where we had a glass of wine. A meeting of directors appointed against Monday at 10 a clock.

Saturday 19 October 1745

Mr Jack calld. Settled my private balance. Also my balance as cashier, having sett the whole of it into the iron chest, except A Brown's two bags of silver which ly by me in my own house. Gave Mr Shairp £5 silver for bank note. Gave Mr William Monro £10 silver for Lord Monzie's cash draght on Bank. Sent Bank minutes to Mr John Hamilton to revise, Mr Coutts having revised them already. Dined with E[arl of] B[readalbane] and Mr J[ohn] Murray at Abbey. Deliverd up all receipts I had from Finlay Murray for money advancd him for E[arl of] B[readalbane]. Returnd in a chair. Was calld upon after my return from the Abbey by one of Lord Tinwald's house maids to tell that a son of Rollo of Powhouse was searching for arms at that lodging and at Lord Monzie's, on which I went immediatly down, found him and his possie at Lord Tinwald's searching every corner, but he found nothing, he had a highlander guarding the door with a drawn sword, from whom with difficulty I got access. Lord Monzie's housemaid told me, they had taken two small swords out of Lord Monzie's per receipt, which she deliverd to me. Wrote to Lord Monzie under Lieutenant James Campbell's cover, and acquainted him of the above search.

Sunday 20 October 1745

No sermon. Had a letter from Lord G[lenorchy] per McDiarmid dated [ ] with one inclosed for Lady G[lenorchy]. Had a letter from Lady G[lenorchy] per post dated 15th with the inclosed for Lord G[lenorchy]. Had a message from E[arl of] B[readalbane] to dine with him, but made my excuse.

Monday 21 October 1745

Messrs Hamilton, Coutts, Shairp and Philp mett at the Bank according to appointment. Went through the forreign bills, and gave signed directions concerning the same. Deliverd to Da[vid] Baillie all the 60 day bills upon receipt in order to protest and req[ues]t them before expiry. His and the Secretary's receipts standing already for the former parcells in his hands. Pat Smyth, brother to Methven, made a demand in the Prince's name, for payment of £1,819 R[oyal] Bank notes in current coin ... and Wednesday at 12 a clock, and took instruments thereupon in hands of [ ] Watson notary before Andrew Porteous of Burnfoot and Andrew Swan indeweller in Edinburgh witnesses. This demand was immediatly notified to the directors, sitting in the Bank office, who orderd that the same should be complyed with. Da[vid] Baillie deliverd me the list of bills received by him from the directors to be taken care of.

Dined with E[arl of] B[readalbane], Messrs William and John Murray at the Abbey. Waited on Broughton that he might appoint an hour for geting payment of Mr Smith's demand and he named about five this evening. Mr John Hamilton returned Bank minutes after perusall. Broughton according to appointment sent his deputy Mr Lumisdean with the R[oyal] Bank notes, which Robert Selkrig received off his hand, and then told over the gold to him amounting to £1819, which he seald up in his bags and carried away with him. Had a bottle of wine. Thereafter I placd the bank notes according to Mr Selkrig's tale and initials to each parcell in iron chest. I got up the protest taken against the Bank from Mr Lumisdean discharged by Mr Murray of Broughton, and as Swan one of the witnesses could not be had to sign the same Mr Lumisdean is to send him to me to morrow for that purpose.

Tuesday 22nd October 1745

Had a letter from St Germans which I answered. Robert Selkrig sorted the parcell of R[oyal] B[ank] notes which I received last night from Mr Lumisdean in order to be cancelld being £1819. <Replied> Sent Mr Alexander Shairp £2 out of one of my own baggs in the iron chest without write. Changd £5 note to Mr McCulloch's clerk for sixpences. Dined at D Andersons with D[avid] Baillie. Answered a letter of Lady Dunstaffnage's. Sorted modern letters etc lying by me. Wrote to Lady G[lenorchy] and sent her date of all my letters from 14 September to 17 October both inclus[ive], and sent a letter from Lord G[lenorchy] to her Ladyship by itself.

Wednesday 23rd October 1745

Received payment of Mr John Philp payment of the £8 he owd me. Gave him £10 in silver out of the Bank balance per draght on Bank of £18, in which is included the above £8. Called at John McKenzie writer about E[arl of] Eglintone's bills in Bank, and bond of corroborate he was to grant for the largest Mr McKenzie not being in town, his clerk Mr Gray told me the bond was signed, and would be deliverd up on Mr McKenzie's return to town next week. And for the bills a letter might be written to E[arl of] Eglintone to the care of the postmaster of Irvine. Calld at William Drummond bookseller and gave him directions to pack up 200 copies of Jack's Conic Sections to be sent to London. Agreable to Mr Jack's desire. Called at Ja[mes] Stirling merchant and desired him to draw out all accounts I owe him for my self or others. Dined at home s[olus]. Went through the directors' orders concerning the forreign bills, in consequence of which I wrote to the following persons per letter book vizt.

    G[eorge] Middleton and Company
    Earl of Eglintone
    Sir William Maxwell of Sprinkele
    Andrew Chalmer writer for Sir Ja[mes] Dalrymple
    John Sinclair writer
    Hercules Skinner merchant in Montrose
    Lord Rosse
all bearing tomorrow's date and to be then dispatchd per post.

Thursday 24th October

A further demand was this morning early made by Mr Lumisdean in name of the Prince for the sum of £1117 to be paid in current coin in exchange for notes. The foregoing demand I immediatly notified to Messrs Hamilton and Philp, who came to the Bank at a call, who agreed to comply, and Mr Lumisdean has appointed 6 at night for receiving the money. Read all the letters to the directors which I wrote to sundry debtors per order of which they approved. Had a letter from Lady G[lenorchy] dated the 19th with one inclosed (with no address) to be sent off as soon as possible. Had a letter from Lord M[onzie] desiring to send him the news papers etc. Had a letter from Pendrick about his and Lady Braco's bills to the Bank which I laid before the directors. Had a message from the Old Bank desiring to exchange all our notes in their hands, and in as far as they were short of what we had of theirs would give cash to make up the balance. Wrote to my Lady G[lenorchy] in answer to hers of the 19 which I received this day. Mr Lumisdean came and got £1117 in gold for R[oyal] Bank notes. Mind that A[lexander] I[nnes] younger get up the protest from him discharged. George Stirling calld this night and supped with me. Indicted a meeting of directors to morrow at 12 a clock about the message from the Old B[ank] etc. A[lexander] Innes senior received payment of a bill on P[eter] and J[ohn] Murdoch's account on Coutts and Company which I discharged. £60. Had a letter from Lord Monzie.

Friday 25th October 1745

Paid McDiarmid 9 shillings which with 6 shillings formerly completes his last journey to Breadalbane. A[lexander] Innes senior breakfasted with me. The accomptant calld at me. Had a letter to Lady Veronica Campbell's burial. Directors met and resolved to exchange 4000 £ notes with Old Bank to morrow. Had a message from O[ld] Bank by Messrs Fairholm and Spence to exchange the notes within the Castle, which I told them could not be complyed with, as the notes we had of theirs were brought from thence. That our directors had agreed to exchange £4000. They signified that they had more than double that sum, and wanted to have specie for the difference to which I could give no answer till I should acquaint the directors. Had a bottle wine at my house with them.

Saturday 26th October 1745

Mungo Roro calld at me and breakfasted. George Stirling came and took leave. Mr Spence calld to tell that the Old Bank directors had agreed to exchange the £4000 notes at Mr Fairholm's house at 2 a clock, which I notified to Mr Selkrig that he might attend. Mr Kinloch's servant maid came to acquaint me that her master's house at Bruntfield Links was robbd and pillaged last night by 15 highlanders and 2 women, but knew none of their names. I beged of Mungo Roro to get all the information he could, and if possible to recover the goods that the rogues might be punished, which he undertook so far as lay in his power. Mr Kinloch's maid is to endeavour to bring me further information. D[avid] Baillie dined with me.

Exchanged £4000 notes with the Old Bank. While at dinner Mr Lumisden sent me a message he was to call in the afternoon, accordingly at 3 a clock he came and protested £417 R[oyal] B[ank] notes, and having afterwards calld I gave him £400 in gold, with which he was satisfied, having restricted his demand to that sum.

Had a letter from Lord Glenorchy dated 23 October with one for Lady Glen[orchy] and another for M[istres]s Gray both which I sent off this night per post. Had a letter from Auchalader who is a dying dated 22nd. Had a letter from Lord M[onzie] dated 25th. Wrote to Lady G[lenorchy] advising her that I had sent a letter to her Ladyship from Lord G[lenorchy] by this night's post, and another to Lady M[istres]s Gray. E[arl of] Breadalbane calld upon me to the Abbey, went down in a chair suppd with his Lordship and Mr John Murray returnd in a chair paid 2 shillings and 1 shilling to the Earl's servant who conducted me backward and forward. My errand was to see Lord G[lenorchy]'s letter that the E[arl] might answer the same which he was to do to morrow.

Sunday 27 October 1745

No sermon. Went to the Castle deliverd the letters for General Guest from Lord Glenorchy and Governor Alexander Campbell and message from Lord Monzie all about Fassiefern, but the General would not give answers in writing, only verbally that he thought the Governor might release him on good bail such as Lord G[lenorchy] approvd of. Returnd to the coffee house. Dined at home s[olus]. Inshewen calld upon me after dinner to whom I deliverd Auchalader's letter about his son Peter. Letters came to me from the Abbey for my dispatching Anderson to Taymouth. Answered Lord Glenorchy's letter of 16 and 23 October and sent him in a by cover Courant 24 and Mercury 25 October. Also letter to a gentleman in England from one in the Prince's army. I further sent his Lordship the general evening post and addrresses of Lords and Commons these three last me to se[n]d to Lord M[onzie]. Answered Lord Monzie's letters of 23 and 25 October and sent him inclosed in a by cover the three English prints mentioned within, with Courants 4 and 7 October (per special direction) Courant 24 and Mercury 25 October and letter to a gentleman in England from one in the Prince's army. All per John Anderson. Sent Lord Glenorchy likewise by him half pound fine green tea from James Stirling and a cannister which late I bought. Sent letter to Coulteraller from [   ] per his clerk. Sent Lord G[lenorchy] under cover two letters from my Lady whereof one not addresst and bond to be signd by his Lordship and me to Mr John Murray for £100 of which his Lordship is to relieve me. Answered Auchalader's letter of the 22nd.

Monday 28th October 1745

Had a visit from Stewart of Ballachelies about the debt due by him and the deceast John Stewart mess[enge]r to me by bond. Had a letter from Mr John Hamilton desiring to call a meeting of directors ordinary and extraordinary to consider of a letter to him from Provost Coutts about Bank affairs. Gave directions to the porter to summond a court accordingly this day at 3 afternoon. Waited upon upon Lady

Dunstaffnage and gave her £3 in silver for which and £2.1. I advancd her formerly without receipt I took her bill on Inveraw in part of her annuities.

Court of directors ordinary and extraordinary

Present

Ordinary	Extraordinary
Mr Hamilton	Mr Hathorn
Mr Shairp	Mr Forbes
Mr Philp	Mr Mansfield

Had under consideration a letter from Mr Coutts to Mr Hamilton advising that upon a conversation with the Lord Justice Clerk about Bank affairs his Lordship had found fault with almost every part of the directors' conduct, but had not time to give the particulars. As the directors were not sensible of any one article of misconduct, they delayed saying any thing further of that matter 'till Mr Hamilton should have another letter from Provost Coutts. The Cashier reported that he had exchangd £4000 Old B[ank] notes for new, and as he had now only a small sum more on hand wanted to know whether 'twas proper to endeavour to get any more, because that the Old Bank had still a considerable sum of our notes in their hands. It was the opinion of the meeting that as many Old notes as possible should be got, and that they themselves should contribute what they could that way. It was further their opinion that in case any after demand should be made upon the bank by the P[rince] within £2,000, that the same should be answerd as formerly, and that the ordinary directors should take the same out of the Castle. Agreed to take payments from Mr Coutts of the 4,000 £ Bank money in his hands, as money comes in to him, but that his partner should be told that specie or Old Bank notes would be more acceptable. Made up Bank minutes to this day. Poem.

Tuesday 29th October 1745

Mr Fisher of Inveraray calld upon me about Inveraw's daughter's homegoing. Went with him to Mrs Campbell in the Canongate, where we agreed that 'twas proper to send the child home with Mr Fisher, 'till the troubles be some how abated. Signed a discharge on a Bank bill which Mr Selkrig received the contents of. Had a letter from Lady G[lenorchy] dated the 24th, with one inclosed for Lord Glenorchy, both were opend on the road, but sealed again. Had a letter from Lord Rosse holding the two bills sent us by G[eorge] Middleton and Company as good as accepted. Gave Mr Shairp gold for £16 old and new bank notes. Had a confusd story of a forgery of the Royal Bank notes, which was told him by John Bisset, whom I sent for, and he's to bring all the information he can get. Dined at home s[olus]. Wrote to Mr Mathias per letter book. Wrote to Clathick. Answered Lady Glenorchy's of the 24th October thanked her for hint about Equivalent Company's murmuring. John Comrie calld upon me. A[lexander] Innes yo[unge]r deliverd me the two last protests which he received from Mr Lumisden dischargd. Settled accompts with John Yule late ploughman at Finlarig, and gave him £1.10 in part of his wages, he not inclining to take the remainder for fear of robbery. Wrote to St Germans. Poem continued.

Wednesday 30 October 1745

Mr Lumisden made a further demand of £174 to be exchangd tomorrow at 12 a
clock. Sent snuff and paper to E[arl of] Breadalbane. Answered Mr McNachlane's
letter per Mr Dow. Settled my balance in iron chest. J[ohn] Comrie came in to me
after dinner. Likewise Sir John Holburn and Mr William Hogg. Saw Robert Wall
and deliverd Lord Monzie's message. Had about 100 £ from A Brown for R[oyal]
B[ank] notes.

Thursday 31 October

Exchanged some R[oyal] for Old Bank notes with Baillie Mansfield. Had some gold
from the tellers for notes. Waited for Mr Lumesdean to exchange but he did not
call. Dined s[olus]. A[lexander] Innes calld while at dinner. Drew out my account
with Inveraw in order to be sent off by Mr Fisher. Sorted the vouchers. Deliverd
the account to Mr Ewart to calculate the interest. Answered a letter I had from
St Germans by his brother the attorney. A[lexander] Campbell brewer calld at me
about Mungo Roro. Had a letter from P[eter] and J[ohn] Murdoch of 30th. Wrote
to Lady Glenorchy. The P[rince] went this evening to Pinkie.

Friday 1 November 1745

A message from L with whom I saw K[inloc]h. Mr Philp got £190 per draght on cash
account. Sent off letter to St G[ermains] per attorney. Mr Lumisdean calld for £174
in gold for notes of like value, but had not the protest extended, the notary and
witnesses having left the town and Broughton was likewise gone. Mr Ewart sent me
Inveraw's account with calcul of interest. Mr Trotter calld at me from Provost
Coutts to know if I had any message for him, told him the directors were willing to
take what partial payments he could conveniently make. D[ined] s[olus]. Drew out
a second copy of Inveraw's account. Sorted several parcells of letters from St
Germans, in order to put the vouchers of his accompts in order. Highland left this
place wholly today. Archibald McDiarmid in Inshewen in Glenlochay lodged £30
with me for which I granted him receipt to be accountable to Auchalader for the
same on demand.

Saturday 2nd November 1745

Accomptant calld upon me. Ja[mes] Niccol watchmaker in Cannongate calld and
deliverd me for safety a gold chesst watch and two chagreen cases, besides the two
gold cases - J Blackborow London maker no.1640. All which I'm to deliver to him
on demand. Busy all day sorting and tottling my old pocket cash books and
memoranda books in order to place them according to their dates. Wrote to Lady
Glenorchy that the highland army was gone southward. Wrote same to Lord
Glenorchy. Also to Lord Monzie. Both these last letters I sent under cover to
Lieutenant Ja[mes] Campbell at Stirling to whom I notified in the general that the

city was thinner than for some weeks past. Sent messages to E[arl of] Breadalbane
and his Lordship had one at me. Sent to Mrs Scott and to Mr Kinloch's house but
none there.

Sunday 3 November

Heard s[ermon] per Mathison new church. Dined with E[arl of] B[readalbane], Sir
Ja[mes] Holburn and J[ohn] M[urray] at Abbey. There received letters per post
vizt: one from Lady G[lenorchy] dated Tuesday 29 October with one inclosed for
Lord G[lenorchy] and in another cover one from Lady Hariot for his Lordship.
Received a letter from Captain Stirling dated 29 October. Received letter from Lord
Monzie dated 1 November. Received letter from Carwhin dated 28 October. Supd
with E[arl of] B[readalbane]. Returnd in a chair.

Monday 4 November 1745

Busy sorting vouchers of St Germans account in order to settle. Had a letter from
the E[arl] of Breadalbane telling me the mob had got up in the Abbey, were opening
doors and like to destroy the house and every thing in it, therefore desiring to apply
to General Guest for a safe guard and to show him his Lordship's letter.
Accordingly I wrote to the General, sent the Earl's letter inclosed by Finlay Moray,
that he might tell the General what he had seen. Finlay Moray returned and told me
the General was immediatly to send down a Guard to the Abbey to protect it.
Remainder of this afternoon adjusting St Germans vouchers.

Tuesday 5 November 1745

Closed Inveraw's account; and added vizt
Post[age] letters	7.4
Commission	3.3.4
Interest per calcul	1.14.6 $^{1}/_{3}$

These three articles to be posted to my ledger per journal entry, by which the
balance due by him to me is 84.9.6 bearing interest from 1 instant. This account
I inclosed in a letter to Inveraw, and sent the same away by Mr Fisher. I wrote at
same time about Lady Dunstaffnage's annuity. Drew out notes for a calcul of
interest on St Germans account. R[obert] Selking received £286 from Mr Coutts
part of his ob[ligation] to the bank for which I signd receipt. Mr Shairp calld and
wrote a letter beside me. Dind at home, St Germans and A Baillie with me. Mr
William Monro calld. Mr Fisher calld and we agreed that Inveraw's daughter
should continue in town at Mrs Campbell. Anderson came to town with letters vizt:
<dated November 2> one from Lord Glenorchy with £100 bond to Mr J[ohn]
Murray (in which I'm to engage); <dated November 4> one from Lord Monzie;
<dated November 3> one from young Auchalader; <November 3> one for Lady
Glenorchy.

Wrote to my Lady Glenorchy and sent Lord Glenorchy's letter to her ladyship by itself . Answered Carwhin's of 28 October and sent lumstall of the payments I made on his bill to the bank; and of E[arl of] Breadalbane's bond to them. Wrote to Captain Stirling. Wrote to Lord Monzie under Lieutenant James Campbell's cover. St Germans supped with me and revised my account current, which he carried with him to look over more fully.

Wednesday 6th November 1745

Mr Kinloch's maid calld upon me for a letter to Mr Glasgow in the Castle to be assisting to her in finding out the things pillaged out of her master's house amongst these carried up to the Castle. Mr Ron[al]d C[raufurd] calld upon me for loan of £200 which I gave him out of my B[ank] balance on his note pay[able] on demand, which I lodged in iron chest. Dined at Abbey with E[arl of] B[readalbane], St Germans and Mr John Murray. I then signed a conjunct bond with Lord Glenorchy to Mr John Murray, son to Lord Edward Murray, for £100 pay[able] at Whitsunday next, and bearing interest from Martinmas next. Twas signed by my Lord Glenorchy on the 2nd instant at Auchmore witness Lochland and young Auchalader, and by me at the Abbay this day, witnesses St Germans and Finlay Murray servant to the Earl of Breadalbane. Nota. Lord Glenorchy by his letter of 2nd instant is to relieve me of this engagement.

I deliverd the bond to Mr Murray who paid me the money, which I'm to remitt to my Lady Glenorchy at London per bill agreable to Lord Glenorchy's directions. St Germans treated me with a coach to the Abbey and back again. Answerd Douchray's letter of 2nd July last. Posted up all my letter book. Supped at home, St Germans with me. The E[arl] of B[readalbane] signed power as one of the exe[cuto]rs of Colonel Fraser's will for Lady Erskine of geting up her father's furniture in Sir Ja[mes] Grant's possession.

Thursday 7th November 1745

Had a letter from Sir William Maxwell promising payment of Sir Alexander Jardin's bills in Bank. Wrote to Lord Monzie per Stirling post under Lieutenant Campbell's cover. Wrote to Lord Glenorchy per Anderson in answer to his Lordship's of the 2nd and sent him two letters from Lady Glenorchy one from Lady Hariot C[ockburn]. A memorandum wrote by Lady G[lenorchy] with £1.7. - inclosed of drink money to be distributed at Taymouth. Sent him sundry Mercurys, Courants and English newspapers inclosed to Lord M[onzie]. Sent him a letter from the Earl. Wrote to Lady Glenorchy and sent her a power to Lady Erskine, by the exe[cutors] of her father's will, to receive his furniture now lying at Sir James Grant's at London. Wrote to G[eorge] Stirling Auchyll at Herbert per Falkirk and sent him his father's last letter to me to be forwarded to his mama. Wrote to young Auchalader and desired him to get 16 shillings for me from Dr McIntyre at the mines. Sent off the letter for Douchray which I wrote yesterday. Sent off a letter from E[arl of] B[readalbane] to Auchalader. Sent a letter left with me for Coulterallers. Sent a letter left with me by young Inshewen for Auchalader. Got Mr Ewart to calculate the interest on St Germans accounts which amounts to £10.11.1.

Friday 8 November 1745

Dispatched Anderson this day with the letters for Lord Glenorchy etc which I wrote last night. Received a letter from Lady G[lenorchy] this morning dated 2nd November and one for Lord Glen[orchy] in another packet, which I dispatched by Anderson with the English newspaper. Wrote to Coulterallers about the debt due to me by Culdairs. Gave Anderson half a crown. Busy drawing out the family of Breadalbane's account. Supped at Mr Scots in Blackfrierwynd.

Saturday 9th November 1745

Lent James Nicolson writer a guinea. Bought a bill of B[aillie] Mansfield for Lady Glenorchy for £100. Exchange £1. French madam cald upon me. Exchanged new for O[ld] Bank notes with B[aillie] Mansfield £200. Dined at E[arl of] B[readalbane]'s with John M[urray]. Paid a visit at Mrs Campbell in Canongate in afternoon. Answered Lady Glenorchy's of the 2nd current, and sent her a bill for £100 drawn by General William Blakeney on Captain Alexander Wilson 8 November at 10 days date indorsd to her Ladyship by Baillie Mansfield value of me. Exchange £1. Wrote to P[eter] and J[ohn] Murdoch per letterbook. Wrote to Lord Monzie about ... and sent Mrs Anderson's certificate inclosed. Wrote to Gleneure, and sent him a copy of his brother Ensign Archibald's letter of 8th September.

Sunday 10th November 1745

Sermon per Kinloch new church. Dined with E[arl of] B[readalbane] and Mr Murray at Abbey. Supped there likewise. Came home about 10 at night.

Monday 11 November 1745

Received sundry letters per post vizt: from Lady Glen[orchy] dated 5 with one for Lord G[lenorchy] agreable to which I'm to make out and send his Lordship a bond for 600 to Mr Yorke to sign.
From Mr Richard Jack.
From Byers.

Paid my account to James Stirling merchant	£10. 8. 7½
Paid my account for Lord Glenorchy tea	£1. 4. -
Paid my account for Auchalader	£4. 5. 8

All stated per cash book. Dined at home s[olus]. Begun to compose some lines. Paid a visit at Mr Kinloch's and paid him the £37 lodged with me by his wife when she left the town 7th October. Finished my composure. Paid a visit at Lady Dunstaffnage's.

Tuesday 12 November 1745

Went to George Gordon's to advise about £600 bond by Lord G[lenorchy] to

Mr Y[orke] and wrote that bond. Exchanged £5 silver for notes with Mr Shairp. Tellers came to the office. Dined s[olus]. Went after dinner to Luckie Clerks to see Messrs Whitefoord and Graham. Wrote to Lord Glen[orchy] and sent him the above bond to sign, also a letter from my Lady. Wrote to Lord Monzie and sent Lord Glenorchy's packet inclosed. All under cover to Lieutenant James Campbell per Wright at Monzie. Wrote to Lady Glen[orchy]. Wrote to Byers. Wrote to Captain Stirling and sent him a letter from his son. Received letters from Miss Jeany Stirling. Also one from her brother with copies of another due by Herbertshire on which he's pursued. Wrote to Captain Stirling and sent him a letter from his son with proxy for serving him heir to his brother cum beneficio, also a factory to his son on estate of Herbertshire. Wrote to Eq[uivalen]t Company per letter book. Wrote to Mr Ja[mes] Mathias. Wrote to G[eorge] Middleton and Company per letter book.

Wednesday 13 November 1745

Despatched George Stirling's letter and sent him Mrs Young's and George Cuningham's account. Wrote to Miss Jeany and sent her gloves and snuff and returnd her key. Paid Lord Glenorchy's landry maid £4.10 of wages per disch[arge]. Mr William Monro calld. Exchanged new for old notes with Baillie M[ansfield] £215. Alexander Chalmers calld with message from Mr Alison. Made out sundry notes from E[arl of] B[readalbane]'s account in order to cast up the interest. St Germans supped with me. This day the judges enterd the City in procession.

Thursday 14 November 1745

Deliverd notes of E[arl of] B[readalbane]'s accounts to Mr Ewart to calculate the interest which he did. Tellers came to the office and received payment of Mollysons bill and a sum from Provost Coutts for both which I signd discharges. Waited upon Provost Coutts per message and had a conversation about Bank affairs, he's to go out of town not to return till 21 unless sent for. Dined s[olus].

Wrote a disch[arge] by Lady Dunstaffnage for her last half years annuity which I paid her, discompting £17.1.- which she owd me per bills which I deliverd up. Sum paid her was £19.1.2 2/3 to complete the 650 monthly restricted annuity. Had a meeting with Mr Da[vid] Kinloch. Went to the Abbey in chair and staid with E[arl of] B[readalbane] about an hour and he has appointed us to be with him to morrow by 12 a clock. Returned in chair a boisterous night. 2000 foot and dragoons enterd the City this evening. Wrote to Lady Glenorchy. Wrote to Lord M[onzie] under Lieutenant C[ampbell]'s cover. St Germans and D[avid] Kinloch suppd with me.

Friday November 15 1745

Mr Whitefoord calld upon me also Principal Campbell of Glasgow who breakfasted with me. Mr Tulloch calld to notify that his grandson Peter had got an Ensign etc.

Mr David Kinloch calld, went with him to the Abbey presented him to the Earl of
Breadalbane at the Abbey. Had letters from Lord Glenorchy with three for the post
horse for London. Had letter from Lord Monzie. Sir John Inglis told me he had
dispatched the letter for Lady Glenorchy deliverd to him by Sir Charles Gilmore's
servant. Dined at home St Germans with me. Wrote an appology to E[arl of]
B[readalbane] that I could not wait upon him 'till to morrow at dinner. Wrote to
Spalding as Lord M[onzie] desired. Wrote to Robert Wall to come to me to morrow
that I might pay him for commission of Lieut[enancy]. Sorted sundry letters in my
office. St Germans came home and suppd.

Saturday November 16 1745

J[ohn] Grahame breakfasted with me. Got letter from Lord Monzie per Stirling
post and one inclosed for Lord Justice Clerk which I deliverd in at the lodging, and
on seing his Lordship afterwards found he had received it, but he gave no answer.
Calld on Mr Whitefoord. Saw Denovan. Dined with E[arl of] B[readalbane] and
J[ohn] M[urray] at Abbey. E[arl of] Breadalbane deliverd me his discharge of
annuity from Lammas to Martinmas last, on which I gave him my note for £30 on
demand. Returnd to town in the afternoon. G[eorge] Innes calld on me. Paid a visit
to Mrs H. Came home. Wrote to Lord M[onzie] per Stirling and sent R Watt's answer.
Wrote to Lady Glenorchy and told there were 3 letters from her Lord <whereof>
one to her Ladyship, one for Lady Harriot and one for Lady Grey or Mr Yorke.
Wrote to Lordship G[lenorchy] one letter about his own business and another about
Mr K[inloc]h. NB. These two last not sent away 'till Monday 18th the servant
having waited till the arrival of Sunday's post which did not come in till Monday.

Sunday

Heard sermon in new church. Dined s[olus]. Went to Mr Whitefoord's after
sermons. From thence down to the Abbey where I supd with E[arl of] B[readalbane].

Monday 18 November 1745

Wrote to Lord J[ustice] Clerk about Bank affairs and advised him the Old Bank
had opend shop. Got his Lordship's answer by Ja[mes] Lyon on which I indicted a
meeting of ordinary directors to morrow at 12 a clock. Orderd all the bank officers
to attend that a state of affairs might be made up. Advised Mr Whitefoord of the
above. Dined s[olus]. Got letter from Lady Glen[orchy] with one for her Lord and
another for him from Lady Harriot [Cockburn]. Got letter from Mr Middleton.
Also one from Mr Mathias. And one under his cover for Lord M[onzie] marked by
Clathick. Got a letter from Captain Stirling. Wrote to Lord Glen[orchy] per
Anderson and sent him the letters from Lady G[lenorchy], Lady H[arriot
Cockburn], Carwhin's nephew, one I had from Peter Hepburn and one from the
Earl. Sent him a parcel of Scots and English news papers. Wrote him a long letter
about Da[vid] K[inloc]h. Wrote Lord M[onzie] and sent him Lord Justice Clerk's
inclosed, also Spalding's letter and the above marked by Clathick. Sent all Lord

Glenorchy's newspapers and magazine under his Lordship's cover.

Tuesday 19 November 1745

Ballanced my Bank cash which held right. Attended a meeting of directors per minute. Waited on General Guest and lady with Lady Glen[orchy]'s compliments. Saw George Cheap there. Dined with E[arl of] B[readalbane] being his Lordship's birthday when he enterd 84. J[ohn] Murray solus. Gave servant 7 shillings. Returnd home in the afternoon. Answered Lady Glen[orchy]'s letter of the 12th and advised that the highlanders had taken Carlisle. Wrote the same to Lord Monzie. Received a letter from Lady Glenorchy of the 14 which I answered in the above. Ar[chibal]d McNab of Neton lodgd £50 with me for Auchalader per receipt by the hands of James Muirhead merchant in Edinburgh.

Wednesday 20 November 1745

Went to the castle of Edinburgh with severall of the officers of the Bank and got down all the boxes belonging to the accomptants office being 18 in number. Paid sundrys as per account at the castle etc. A meeting of directors at 12 a clock present Messrs Hamilton and Shairp. Mr Whitefoord read them a memorandum about Bank affairs. Settled my Bank balance in part. D[avid] Baillie dined with me. William Fraser calld about a draght of Captain Thynne which could not be answered till the Bank opens.

Thursday 21 November 1745

Received letter from Lady Glenorchy of 16th which I answerd and sent one to Miller about the goods aboard the Elizabeth for London. Sundry more boxes got down from the castle belonging to the Bank. Settled with the letters and likewise my own balance in Bank. Mind to send off letter to Lord G[lenorchy] from my Lady. Drew memorandum about Bank affairs from one of Mr Whitefoord's with which he waited on Lord Justice Clerk. Wrote to Captain Stirling at Forrests coffee house. Wrote to his Lady and sent her his letter inclosed. I sent these under cover to G[eorge] Stirling at Herbertshire. Wrote to Lord Monzie telling the directors wanted him greatly to town. This was under Lieutenant Ja[mes] Campbell's cover. Wrote to G[eorge] Middleton.

Friday 22 November 1745

Meeting of directors per minute. Busy making out 20 shilling notes. Tho[mas] Tulloch dined with me. Received letter from D[avid]Kinloch which I answered.

Saturday 23 November 1745

Meeting ordinary directors at 10 a clock. Ditto of ordinary and extraordinary at 11 a clock. Struck 3 books 20 shilling notes. Got down rest of Bank effects from castle. Also three boxes of Lord Glenorchy's plate. Made out memorandum for Mr Philp wheresd he was to wait on B Arbuthnot. Auchlyne dined with me. Received letter from Mr McNachlane. McGrigor arrived from Taymouth but broght only a broke up letter from my Lord for Lady Glen[orchy] and cover of a letter for Lord Chancellor and cover of one for me <inclosing £10 bond to Mr Yorke> the letters themselves being taken out by the highlanders on the road. Received two letters from Lord M[onzie] per Mr Fergusson. Wrote to Lady Glen[orchy] and sent her my Lord's broke open letter and his £600 bon[d] to Mr Yorke. Sent off a letter from Lord Monzie for Lord Tinwald under Mr P Craufurd's cover to be left at Mr Middleton's.

Sunday

Monday

Tuesday 26 November

Wrote to Lady Glenorchy. Wrote to Mathias two letters in one of which was a bill for £2000. Wrote to Mr Middleton with bill for £6000.

Wednesday

Thursday

Wrote to Mr Mathias two letters in one of which a bill for £700. Wrote to Captain John Menzies. Wrote to Lord M[onzie] under cover to Lieutenant James Campbell. Wrote to Captain Stirling. Wrote to Mr Merveillieux.

Friday

Saturday 30 November 1745

Got Lord Glenorchy two large chests with his plate out of the castle of Edinburgh where they had been lodged with the Bank's treasure, having got down the three small boxes before, these three are lodged in my cash closet, and the two large ones are in my man servant's room below stairs. Got letter from Lord Glenorchy, also letters from him for

Lady Glenorchy
Lady Harriot
Lord Chancellor
Mr Yorke

all sent off this night.

Dined at Abbey with E[arl of] B[readalbane] and J[ohn] M[urray]. Gave my note to the Earl for £100 on which he granted discharge of his annuity from Martinmas last to Candlemas next. Drew out my accounts with Auchalader sent them to him signed with all the vouchers. Balance in my favour £7 odd. McIntyre schoolmaster at Morinesh's sallary lodged in my hands £2.5 stated to Auchalader's credite. Wrote to D[avid] Kinloch. Wrote to Lady Glenorchy and sent my Lord's letter to her and

59

to Lady Harriot inclosed and one for the C[hancello]r and Mr Yorke by them per covers. Waited upon Col[onel] Whitefoord. Had a letter from McNachlane, with one inclosed for Lochlane from his sister to be sent off. Had a letter from Inveraw.

Sunday

Sermon in new church. Was with E[arl of] B[readalbane] all the evening. Received letter from Lady G[lenorchy] of 26 with two for my Lord. Also one from Lady H[arriot].

Monday 2nd December 1745

Sent Lady Dunstaffnage two volumes of Nisbet's herauldry to be returnd on demand. Answered Lord Glenorchy's letter of the 27th and sent him 3 letters from my Lady, one from Lady Harriot, one from the Chancellor and one from the Earl. Sent him likewise $\frac{1}{2}$ pound fine green tea.

Tuesday

Miss Jeanie Stirling came here.

Wednesday

Thursday 5th December 1745

Received letter from Lady G[lenorchy] dated 30 November which I answerd, also that of 26th November. Had a letter then from her for his Lord, one from Mr Yorke for him and one for Thomson at Taymouth, all to be sent off. Answered Lord Tinwald's letter, and sent his to Lord Monzie. Got letter from Captain Stirling which I answered, and am to send one from him for his Lady as I sent him one from her. Answered Mr Middleton's letter. Got letter from Carwhin with bills for £163.16.8.

PEOPLE AND PLACES MENTIONED IN THE DIARY

The Abbey	The name by which Holyroodhouse, Edinburgh, was then popularly known.
Ardmady	Breadalbane property on the west coast of Argyllshire which had belonged to John Campbell's father.
Auchalader	John Campbell of Auchalader, factor to the Breadalbane Estates, living at Auchmore near the west end of Loch Tay.
Auchlyne	Campbell of Auchlyn (near Auchmore), a Breadalbane Campbell.
David Baillie	Accountant to The Royal Bank of Scotland.
Robert Barcaldines	The Laird of Barcaldine in Argyllshire.
Bellsmilns (Bell's Mills)	At Slateford on the Water of Leith.
Earl of Breadalbane	John Campbell, 2nd Earl of Breadalbane (1662-1752), the diarist John Campbell's Clan Chief, living at Holyroodhouse, Edinburgh.
Governor Alexander Campbell	Deputy Governor of Fort William.
Ensign Allan Campbell	Prisoner from Lord John Murray's Regiment (the 43rd Highlanders) at the Battle of Prestonpans.
Principal Campbell	Neil Campbell, Principal of the University of Glasgow 1728-61.
Shereff Campbell	Archibald Campbell of Stonefield, Deputy-Sheriff of Argyll.
Carwhin	Captain Colin Campbell of Carwhin, officer in the Argyll Militia in the Government Forces, related to 2nd Earl of Breadalbane and partner with John Campbell in the Marble and Slate Co of Nether Lorn.

Lord Chancellor	Philip Hardwicke, Lord Chancellor of Great Britain.
George Cheap	Collector of Revenue, living at Prestonpans.
Clathick	Campbell laird of Clathick estate, near Comrie, Perthshire.
Mrs Clerk	Vintner in Fleshmarket Close, Edinburgh, known like many of the city's female tavern keepers as 'Lucky' Clerk.
Lady Hariot Cockburn	Daughter of 1st Earl of Breadalbane.
General Cope	Lieutenant General Sir John Cope, Commander-in-Chief of the Government Forces in Scotland.
Coulterallers	The Menzies laird of Coulterallers in Southern Lanarkshire.
John Coutts	Merchant, former Lord Provost of Edinburgh and ordinary director of The Royal Bank of Scotland 1744-51.
Ronald Craufurd	Writer to the Signet.
Culdairs	Menzies of Culdares, (Jacobite) Perthshire laird.
Lady Dunstaffnage	Wife of Neil Campbell, Captain of Dunstaffnage Castle in Argyllshire.
Easdale	The slate at Easdale was quarried, from 1745 to 1751, by the Marble and Slate Co of Nether Lorn in which John Campbell and Colin Campbell of Carwhin were partners.
Earl of Eglintone	Alexander Montgomerie, 10th Earl of Eglintoun (1722/3-69), an Ayrshire peer.
Fassiefern	John Cameron of Fassifern, brother to Cameron of Lochiel. Refused to join the Jacobite Cause, but was imprisoned in Fort William in 1745.

William Forbes	Town Clerk of Edinburgh and extraordinary director of The Royal Bank of Scotland 1743-55.
Gladsmuir	Name by which the Battle of Prestonpans was known to Jacobites.
Lady Glenorchy	Arabella Campbell (nèe Pershall), second (English) wife of Lord Glenorchy, resident in London in 1745.
Lord Glenorchy	John Campbell (1695/6-1782), son and heir to 2nd Earl of Breadalbane whom he succeeded as 3rd Earl in 1752.
Glenoure	Colin Campbell of Glenure, Argyllshire (victim, in 1752, of the Appin Murder).
General Guest	Lieutenant General Joshua Guest (1660-1747), left in command at Edinburgh Castle of such Government Forces as remained there in the autumn of 1745.
John Hamilton	Writer to the Signet and ordinary director of The Royal Bank of Scotland 1740-56.
Hugh Hathorn	Merchant in Edinburgh and extraordinary director of The Royal Bank of Scotland 1744-56.
Herbertshire	Near Denny in Stirlingshire, place of residence of the family of Captain Stirling, a naval officer.
Alexander Innes	Teller to The Royal Bank of Scotland.
George Innes	Second cashier and chief teller to The Royal Bank of Scotland 1745-77.
Inshewen	Lieutenant McNabb of Inishewan in the Duke of Perth's (Jacobite) Regiment.
John's coffee house	In Parliament Close, Edinburgh.
William Keir	Baxter (baker) in Edinburgh and extraordinary director of The Royal Bank of Scotland 1743-52.

David Kinloch

Writer to the Signet in Edinburgh, son of Francis Kinloch of Gilmerton.

King's Park

Adjacent to Holyroodhouse, Edinburgh.

Lochiel

Donald Cameron the younger of Lochiel (c.1700-48), acting chief of Clan Cameron and Jacobite Governor of Edinburgh in 1745.

Earl Loudoun's Regiment

Loudoun's Highlanders, raised by the government in the summer of 1745 before the Rising began.

Lovat

Simon Fraser, 12th Lord Lovat (1667-1747). Wavered in the early stages of the Rising, but eventually joined Prince Charles Edward. Executed 1747.

Lumisdean

Andrew Lumisdean, on Murray of Broughton's staff in the Highland Army.

William Mckewan

Public notary in Edinburgh.

Captain McNabb

Son to Laird of McNab and Captain in Loudoun's Highlanders, captured at the Battle of Prestonpans.

Baillie James Mansfield

Merchant in Edinburgh and extraordinary director of The Royal Bank of Scotland 1744-52.

James Mathias

Secretary of the Equivalent Company in London. The company, set up to dispense the pecuniary 'Equivalent' paid to Scotland after the Act of Union 1707, was the precursor of The Royal Bank of Scotland.

Mathison

Reverend John Mathieson (1679-1752), Dean of the Chapel Royal since 1735.

Sir William Maxwell

Laird of Springkell, Dumfriesshire.

George Middleton and Co

Goldsmiths of Strand, London, founded 1692. Later known as Coutts & Co.

Lord Milton	Andrew Fletcher, Lord Justice Clerk and pillar of the Hanoverian establishment in Scotland. Deputy-Governor of The Royal Bank of Scotland 1737-66.
Lord Monzie	Patrick Campbell, a Breadalbane Campbell, Senator of the College of Justice and ordinary director of The Royal Bank of Scotland 1727-51.
Morinesh	Morenish at the west end of Loch Tay, near Killin, Perthshire.
P and J Murdoch	Peter and John Murdoch, tobacco merchants in Glasgow.
John Murray	Associate at Holyroodhouse of 2nd Earl of Breadalbane.
John Murray of Broughton	Secretary to Prince Charles Edward in the '45, captured in 1746, but pardoned on turning king's evidence against Lord Lovat.
Old Bank	Bank of Scotland, at Old Bank Close on the north side of the Lawnmarket, Edinburgh.
John Philp	Auditor in the Exchequer in Edinburgh and ordinary director of The Royal Bank of Scotland 1727-51, living at Greenlaw, Midlothian.
Pinkie	House near Musselburgh of the Marquis of Tweeddale, Secretary of State for Scotland.
Pleasants	The Pleasance, suburb of Edinburgh, just outside the city walls.
General Preston	General George Preston (c.1659-1748), Deputy Governor of Edinburgh Castle in 1745.
The Prince	Prince Charles Edward Stuart (1720-88), eldest son of James III and VIII. Born and educated in Rome and landed in Scotland in August 1745 to raise a Jacobite army to oust the Hanoverians from the British throne.

Rollo of Powhouse

A Stirlingshire laird, two sons of whom served with the Jacobite Army.

Mungo Roro

Captain McGregor of Roro (in Glenlyon), of the Atholl Brigade in the Jacobite Army.

Lord Rosse

George Ross, 13th Lord Ross (1681-1754), Commissioner of Customs and Salt.

Royal Burrows

Royal Burghs of Scotland.

St Germans

James Campbell of St Germains in East Lothian, friend of John Campbell.

Alexander Shairp

Merchant in Edinburgh and ordinary director of The Royal Bank of Scotland 1743-73.

Peter Smith

Brother to the Laird of Methven (near Perth), on Murray of Broughton's staff.

Stewart of Ballachelies

Alexander Stewart of Ballachulish (in Appin), whose son was serving with the Appin Regiment of the Jacobite Army.

Taymouth

Taymouth Castle at the east end of Loch Tay.

Lord Tinwald

Charles Areskine, Senator of the College of Justice and extraordinary director of The Royal Bank of Scotland 1727-64.

Turnbull's

Mrs Turnbull's tavern near the Tron Kirk, Edinburgh.

Tymdrum

Tyndrum, in the hills of West Perthshire.

Weigh House

Building at the head of the Lawnmarket occupied by the Jacobite Army while besieging Edinburgh Castle.

Alan Whitefoord

General Receiver of Land Tax, cashier of The Royal Bank of Scotland 1727-45 and ordinary director of the Bank 1746-61.

Colonel Whitefoord

Taken prisoner from Cope's army at the Battle of Prestonpans, later released on parole.

INDEX